CO 1 64 58450 69

C000099770

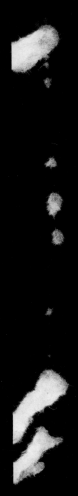

TOM PAINE

The Life of a Revolutionary

Harry Harmer

First published in Great Britain in 2006 by
Haus Publishing Limited
26 Cadogan Court
Draycott Avenue
London SW3 3BX

www.hauspublishing.co.uk

Copyright © Harry Harmer, 2006

The moral right of the author has been asserted

A CIP catalogue record for this book
is available from the British Library

ISBN 1-904950-24-8

Typeset in Caslon by MacGuru Ltd
info@macguru.org.uk

Printed and bound by Graphicom in Vicenza, Italy

Jacket image: Mary Evans Picture Library

CONDITIONS OF SALE
All rights reserved. No part of this publication may be reproduced,
stored in a retrieval system, or transmitted in any form or by any
means, electronic, mechanical, photocopying, recording or
otherwise, without the prior permission of the publisher

This book is sold subject to the condition that it shall not, by way of trade
or otherwise, be lent, re-sold, hired out or otherwise circulated without
the publisher's prior consent in any form of binding or cover other than
that in which it is published and without a similar condition including
this condition being imposed on the subsequent purchaser

Durham County Council Cultural & Leisure	
CO 1 64 58450 69	
Askews	
B	

CONTENTS

Introduction 1

1. A moral education 3
2. Enlightenment 7
3. Strictness of duty 11
4. Ingenious young man 15
5. The climate of America 19
6. Thus far a Quaker 23
7. To begin the world over again 28
8. A statue of gold 33
9. The American crisis 37
10. Stranger without connections 41
11. Neither the place nor the people 46
12. Never was a man less beloved 50
13. A great nation 55
14. Bridges and candles 60
15. Reflections on the Revolution 65
16. *Rights of Man*, Part One 69
17. England is not yet free 74
18. *Rights of Man*, Part Two 79
19. Among sanguinary men 85
20. *The Age of Reason* 90
21. Not charity but a right 96
22. I care not a straw 102

Endnotes 107
Further Reading 115
Index 119

For my Father,
who introduced me to Tom Paine and the
Rights of Man.

INTRODUCTION

Thomas Paine, always Tom to admirers and enemies alike, is perhaps the most famous unknown figure of the American Revolution, ruthlessly expunged from the history of the birth of the United States while the nation was still young. When the prizes were given out, Paine was always somewhere else, forgotten, refused an invitation to the celebrations. But when the image has faded almost to invisibility, Paine is rediscovered, singing in his optimism, 'We have it in our power to begin the world over again.'[1]

This book describes and examines how a poorly-educated artisan, a failure for the first 37 years of his life in England, blossomed in America into a giant of agitational journalism, galvanizing the colonists to struggle for a democratic republic free from Britain; how, on his return to England, he was threatened with hanging for his rousing call for an end to monarchy, for democracy and the eradication of poverty; how, fleeing to France, he was welcomed as a champion of liberty and equality, then sentenced to death by the Jacobins for opposing the execution of Louis XVI, escaping the guillotine only by chance; how in the United States which he had played a central part in creating (and which he had named), he was vilified and then ignored, pushed from the historical stage for his vigorous denunciation of the dangers of religious fundamentalism.

In 1656, when debates about democracy were raging in the republic that followed the English Civil War, a Cromwellian supporter told Parliament, 'I would not have a people know their own strength.'[2] Paine, the heir to those debates, thought the contrary and pressed that thought on both sides of the Atlantic. The argument continues and Paine refuses to be quiet.

If Paine returned, it is easy to imagine his disappointment that the battles he fought remain to be won. He would find Britain a monarchy, albeit with the monarch's direct political power exchanged for a stifling feudal symbolism; an unelected second chamber in which appointed cronies sit instead of hereditary lords; and the people still with no written constitution as a guarantee of their liberties. In the America he loved, Paine would find a democracy so in thrall to the corporations that the parties seem no more than factions in a one-party state; and the poverty that he hated enmeshed with the racial prejudice that he loathed. Wherever Paine found himself, he instinctively strove to shatter the carapace of deceit that every establishment lays on society, to prod it with his pen until the cracks could no longer be ignored. Paine's words were his life and continue to ring out with anger and hope.

*

My thanks are due to Barbara Schwepcke for inviting me to write this book, and to Chelsey Fox for persistently encouraging me to do so. I must also thank Stephen Chumbley for his courteous efficiency as my editor. My apologies are due to Arianna Silvestri for the lost weekends of a summer in which I put Tom Paine before her, and my gratitude to Tiger Tim for the pleasure of his company.

Harry Harmer

A MORAL EDUCATION

1

Thomas Paine thrust himself into world history on the eve of his 39th birthday in January 1776, rousing the North American colonies to break with Britain. His hope was of an independent republic that would act as a democratic beacon to old Europe. His existence had, until then, been marked by failure, disappointment and unhappiness. Paine described in 1792 how he had had all the inconvenience of early life against him but that in America, 'I saw an opportunity, in which I thought I could do some good, and I followed exactly what my heart dictated. I neither read books, nor studied other people's opinions. I thought for myself.'[1]

Information on the first half of Paine's life is sparse. He wrote no autobiography and the few details he gives in his writings are intended more often to bolster an argument than to reveal his personality. In his fifties, for example, Paine claimed that at about the age of eight he had grasped the fundamental flaw at the heart of Christianity. He described a vivid recollection of walking in a garden after being subjected to a sermon on redemption by the death of the Son of God. Paine wrote of the revulsion he had felt at a god killing his own son and of his conviction that God was 'too good to do such an action, and also too almighty to be under any necessity of doing it'.[2]

A friend of Paine's pointed to a precocious demonstration of a radical sensibility. As an eight-year-old, again, Paine had written a verse on the death of a pet crow that could be read as an awareness of hierarchy and its precariousness:

'Here lies the body of John Crow
Who once was high but now is low;
Ye brother Crows take warning all,
For as you rise, so you must fall.'[3]

Paine was born on 29 January 1737 to Joseph and Frances Pain (née Cocke) in Thetford, Norfolk. (Paine added an 'e' to his name soon after his arrival in America.) Joseph, a staymaker (a manufacturer of women's corsets) and the owner of a small farm, was relatively lowly though not poor. His business brought in £30 a year, almost four times what an agricultural labourer was paid. Indeed, Joseph was made a freeman of the town in the year his son was born, a sign that he had acquired some status in the locality. Nevertheless, Paine recalled that his parents had sacrificed themselves to secure him an education.

Paine's mother Frances was 11 years older than Joseph and conscious that, as a lawyer's daughter, she had married beneath herself. One description of Paine's mother is of a 'woman of sour temper and an eccentric character'.[4] She appears to have been undemonstrative, slow in showing affection. While Paine supported her in her old age, he once regretted to an American friend that an unpleasant woman he had recently met reminded him of his mother. Paine found little contentment in his relationships with women, although on paper he would occasionally show an advanced sympathy with their position in society.

Paine was an only child, a sister, Elizabeth, having died shortly after her birth in 1738. The family lived in Bridge Street, a respectable area housing what was, in effect, the lower middle class. Thetford was a market town with 2,000 inhabitants, 70 miles from London and 20 from Norwich, standing at the junction of the rivers Thet and Little Ouse. The town sent two members to the House of Commons, elected by 32 voters according to instructions from the local landowner, the Duke of Grafton, a prominent Whig. The county gallows, the scene of public hangings, stood close by the Pains' home. Thetford would have been in Paine's mind when he wrote that in civilised countries one saw '[A]ge going to the workhouse, and youth to the gallows', and asked, 'Why is it that scarcely any are executed but the poor?'[5]

It is a mark of Paine's ordinariness that so little is known about his family's lives or his boyhood friendships and activities. Paine's father had been a Quaker, a member of the Society of Friends, founded by the dissenter George Fox in the 1650s. The Quakers rejected a paid priesthood and the literal reading of the Bible, believing that God could be experienced by all individuals through an inner light and without mediation. Their refusal to pay tithes, take oaths or defer to social superiors led to their persecution after the restoration of the monarchy in 1660. Joseph had been expelled from the sect for marrying outside, but retained his faith, and Paine noted that his father's Quaker beliefs ensured he enjoyed '[A]n exceedingly good moral education, and a tolerable stock of useful learning', but there is a sense of a Puritan chilliness. Paine praised the sect's philanthropy, though amused himself with the thought '[I]f the taste of a Quaker could have been consulted at the creation, what a silent and drab-coloured creation it would have been! Not a flower would have blossomed its gaieties, nor a bird been permitted to sing'. Paine claimed a talent for poetry, which he had repressed 'as leading too much into the field of imagination'. His mind, he said, had been inclined more towards science.[6]

As a Quaker, Joseph Pain had been born into a Christian sect that within living memory had experienced persecution, imprisonment and exile. His wife, on the other hand, was an Anglican, a member of the established church, a 'patriot' by definition. If her son was to be influenced by his father's Quaker vision, she ensured that he was touched equally by Anglican orthodoxy. Paine was baptized into the Church of England and his aunt, with whom he lived for a period, encouraged him to undergo the ritual of confirmation by the Bishop of Norwich. One writer suggests that Paine ultimately resolved the tensions these divisions caused by rejecting both beliefs, while absorbing what he saw as the best in their moral teachings.[7] In adult life Paine clung, as his writings forcefully show, to the Quaker suspicion of unmerited authority in both religion and politics, holding fast to a confidence that an inner light could lead an individual to the truth. But he had few illusions, writing in 1776, '[W]ere the impulses of conscience clear, uniform, and irresistibly obeyed there would be no need of government'.[8]

In 1744, at the age of seven, Paine began his formal education at Thetford Grammar School, which had a basic curriculum that equipped the sons of artisans and small shopkeepers to meet the growing demand for clerks. The assistant schoolmaster who taught Paine, the Rev. William Knowles, offered extra writing and arithmetic for a small charge, one that

Paine's aunt met. Knowles, who had spent time at sea as chaplain on a man-of-war, entertained the boys with tales of his adventures. Paine was placed in a group that did not learn Latin, Quakers feeling uncomfortable with the language's Roman Catholic connections. He later criticised the teaching of the dead languages, which he said it would be as well to abolish 'and make learning consist, as it originally did, in scientific knowledge'.[9] The school grounded Paine in basic skills that the majority of his contemporaries were unlikely to share, but he was to say that any usefulness formal schooling had lay in the basis it provided for self-education.

Paine left school in 1750 to become an apprentice to his father, apparently destined to follow the path to journeyman and then self-employed master staymaker. For six years Paine underwent the discipline of cutting, shaping and stitching corsets, brooding perhaps on how little opportunity had come from the education for which his family had made such sacrifices. As the apprenticeship came to an end in 1756, Joseph Pain's business fell victim to changes in taste and a decline in the local market. His prospects now even more limited, that summer Paine left Thetford for London.

ENLIGHTENMENT

2

It was at this point that political developments set in train events that would alter Paine's life beyond all expectations. On 28 May 1756, Britain declared war on France, opening a struggle for the domination of North America and India that was to last until 1763 and thus become known as the Seven Years War. The result of the conflict, and its financial cost, would set the course for a struggle by the American colonists against British rule.

It is unclear whether Paine travelled to London with any definite plan, but it must be assumed he found a master to take him on as a journeyman staymaker, though with little enthusiasm on Paine's part. He responded eagerly to an advertisement placed in the *Daily Advertiser* in October 1756 by Captain Death of the privateer *Terrible*. Death urged 'Gentlemen Sailors, and able-bodied Landmen, who are inclinable to try their Fortune, as well as serve their King and Country' to join the ship and sail into action against the French. Paine later recalled that he was, at the age of 19, 'raw and adventurous', inflamed by the schoolmaster Knowles's heroic tales of life on a man-of-war.[1] He answered the advertisement and signed articles of agreement committing himself to serve at sea.

Paine's choice was at odds with his father's pacifist Quaker beliefs, though not with his mother's patriotic Anglicanism. A privateer was a civilian vessel licensed by the government to prey on enemy merchant shipping, a form of legalised piracy demanding the skills of shadowing, stalking and a willingness to threaten or use violence. The government's purpose was to destroy enemy trade, rewarding those who engaged in the enterprise with booty.

The *Terrible* set sail in November, but without Paine. Before the ship left port, his father arrived and dissuaded him from embarking, presumably having tracked Paine down through his contacts in the staymaking trade. Paine later recalled his father's 'affectionate and moral remonstrance', implying that what had been uppermost in Joseph Pain's mind had been the fear that his son was about to abandon Quaker principles.[2] Paine had a lucky escape. The *Terrible* lost 150 men in a bloody engagement with the French in the English Channel, fewer than 20 of the crew surviving the battle.

Having accepted parental authority, reluctantly as events were to show, Paine returned to his trade, though not to Thetford. He was engaged by John Morris, a master staymaker with a shop near Covent Garden, and rented a room nearby. The area was vividly cosmopolitan, ridden with poverty, criminality and vice, offering sights and experiences far removed from Thetford's relative tranquillity. But the hours in Morris's shop were long, from six in the morning till eight at night. Unable to endure this for more than a few weeks, Paine sought escape again.

On 17 January 1757 the privateer *King of Prussia* slipped out of London towards the open sea, *en route* to the Caribbean to harry French shipping. The vessel was a substantial man-of-war, with two gun decks and a crew of 250, among them Paine. No experience or even the rudiments of seamanship were required. As Paine later remarked, only 20 of the men on board were trained sailors. He observed that '[A] few able and social sailors will soon instruct a sufficient number of active land-men in the common work of a ship'.[3] Within weeks the *King of Prussia* had seized two prizes, going on in a seven-month expedition to capture in all nine ships and their cargoes. Paine brushed with danger several times, acquiring an un-Quakerish familiarity with the use of violence. The ship's commander, Captain Mendez, recorded that Paine was actively engaged in combat on three occasions. On 20 August the ship docked at Dartmouth in Kent. Paine's share of the voyage's proceeds amounted to £30, a substantial sum for a man who had earned 2s 6d a week as a journeyman. Paine hurried to London, taking lodgings near Covent Garden once more.

Paine, clearly unhappy with life as a staymaker, took the opportunity his earnings from privateering had provided to build on the small capital of his education and follow his interest in science. He spent the autumn and winter of 1757–8 encountering the Enlightenment, the sense of optimism growing in Europe that men and women could, through the exercise of reason, perceive a natural law and a universal order. Paine began his journey by paying two guineas for private classes in the use of globes taught by James Ferguson. Ferguson, a Scottish astronomer, manufactured and sold globes in the Strand, painted portraits, and was an influential populariser of scientific principles. Among his closest friends was Benjamin Franklin, an American representing the colony of Pennsylvania in Europe.

Both Ferguson and Benjamin Martin, the editor of the *General Magazine of Arts and Sciences*, gave public lectures on Newtonian science at a hall near the Strand, which Paine attended for six months, buying a set of globes and making contact with, among others, Dr John Bevis, an astronomer and Fellow of the Royal Society. The English physicist and mathematician Isaac Newton had developed the intellectual framework not only for modern science and systematic experimental method but, by extension, for a fresh way of perceiving a world placed in a harmonious universe. Newton's work encouraged a demand for the application of rational principles to religion, politics, history and economics. Paine had found his future.

Perhaps as valuable to Paine as the encounter with ideas, was the opportunity to meet individuals who, like himself, were seeking an explanation of the world and their place in it. Much of the audience at the lectures given by Ferguson and Martin comprised Dissenting artisans and small shopkeepers, people from Paine's background, who because of their class, beliefs or sex were denied any significant part in public life or influence over events. In this atmosphere, grasping the meaning of the new world opened every orthodoxy to contestation. The fault of mankind lay not in their souls, but in their understanding. Martin's description of God as the 'Omnipotent Architect' demonstrated how far developing scientific knowledge challenged the basic tenets of revealed religion. If the world, the universe, was ordered by natural law, and that law was open to investigation and comprehension through science, then, Paine and those like him would ask, could not the political and social order itself be questioned and, once understood, transformed?

But Paine, as the money from his exploits dwindled, was faced with the more immediate task of earning a living. On the advice of Morris, his former employer, Paine left London for Dover, where he worked as a staymaker for a year. Then, having borrowed £12 from his employer, he moved along the coast to Sandwich where he intended to set up in business for himself. Paine opened trading as a master staymaker in New Street in April 1759, beginning what he must have hoped would be a secure life, with the leisure to develop his scientific interests. Within six months, happiness was added to this. On 27 September Paine married Mary Lambert, an orphan and maid to the wife of a local wool draper.

It has been suggested that Paine became a Methodist preacher in Sandwich, but the evidence is not altogether convincing. Paine made no reference to this in his writings, in particular his spirited denunciation of organised religion, *The Age of Reason*. Indeed, he was to write that it was immoral for any man to make a living out of religion. But Paine may have preferred to forget that he had once preached such a decidedly evangelical form of Christianity as Methodism. An argument in support of the suggestion that he had practised as a preacher was the intimate knowledge of the Old and the New Testaments that he displayed in his writing.

Whatever personal happiness Paine had found, his business soon faced difficulties, with debts mounting. Paine and his wife fled from his creditors to Margate, ten miles from Sandwich. Here, early in 1760, Mary died. There were accusations that Paine had neglected her and that she had died in labour, losing their child. The sadness, and perhaps remorse, that Paine experienced were to colour the rest of his life. One biographer sees in the intensity of the guilt that Paine felt an explanation for his future 'outwardly asexual existence'; another considers that Paine's idealised memories of the wife who had been so suddenly taken from him held him aloof from any other woman.[4] At the age of 23, Paine was beginning his life again.

STRICTNESS OF DUTY

3

Paine's decision was to work for the government as an Excise officer, a tax collector for the Crown. The ironies of this choice would become apparent in later years. For the moment, Paine was seeking financial security. He may also have hoped that the solitary nature of the work offered independence of action, and perhaps satisfy the taste for adventure he had shown in becoming a privateer. Paine was to be disappointed, writing later of the way in which the system wore down the Excise officer's initial enthusiasm. He regretted that '[G]ay ideas of promotion soon expire. The continuance of work, the strictness of duty, and the poverty of the salary, soon beget negligence and indifference'.[1]

The Excise officer's task was to collect customs duties on a range of goods including beer, wine, spirits, tobacco, salt and soap, checking the stocks of publicans and shopkeepers. Pay was poor, a newly-employed officer discovering that the promised £50 a year was subject to deductions for taxes, accommodation and the upkeep of a horse. The figure of the Excise officer was widely unpopular, a fact of which Paine could hardly have been ignorant.

Paine returned to his parents' home in Thetford to prepare for the necessary examination. Having demonstrated to the authorities that he was sober, able to write and calculate, and that he was a confirmed member of the Church of England (a requirement for all Crown posts), Paine took instruction from local Excise officers in the routines of checking goods, making records and compiling reports. After satisfying a supervising officer of his proficiency, Paine had to resort to patronage to find a member of the Commissioners for Excise who would secure him a post. Paine in all likelihood called on his maternal grandfather, a lawyer, to persuade the Duke of Grafton, the local landowner, to act as his patron. On his appointment Paine swore an oath before a Justice of the Peace acknowledging George III as the rightful monarch. Paine would later describe the King as a 'sottish, stupid, stubborn, worthless, brutish man'.[2]

On 1 December 1762 Paine began work gauging brewers' casks in Grantham, Lincolnshire. On 8 August 1764 he was promoted and stationed in Alford, on the North Sea coast, collecting revenues on tea and coffee and keeping watch for smugglers carrying gin from Holland. Paine's career appeared to be progressing well until he fell into a practice widespread among Excise officers, stamping goods and making an official record without carrying out the obligatory checks. Paine may have preferred to spend more time on his continuing interest in science than on his duties. On 13 August 1765 Paine admitted in a letter to the Commissioners that on 11 July he had stamped a victualler's stocks without examining them. He was dismissed on 29 August.

With no choice but to return to the trade he had struggled to avoid, the 28-year-old Paine found work as a journeyman staymaker in Norfolk, moving in 1766 to Lincolnshire for a short period. But he seemed determined to return to the Excise. In the summer Paine travelled to London and on 3 July presented what he described as a 'humble petition' to the Commissioners asking to be restored to his post. A little over a week later the Board of Excise wrote to Paine promising re-appointment when a vacancy arose.

Paine now showed his versatility and persuasiveness by convincing the proprietor of a boys' academy, Mr Noble, of his ability to act as a teacher of English. The £25 a year stipend, half the wage of an Excise officer, showed the profession's relatively low status. The contract with Noble expired in January 1767, but Paine secured another post at a school in Kensington. He renewed his contact with James Ferguson, whose lectures he had attended ten years previously. Ferguson introduced him to the American Benjamin Franklin. Franklin's interest, flattering to Paine but for now of little significance, would later transform his life.

In May 1767 Paine was offered an Excise post in Cornwall, which he declined. A few months later a vacancy came up in the market town and port of Lewes in Sussex where, after a brief visit to his parents in Thetford, Paine began work in February 1768. It is in Lewes that the Paine the world knows began to take recognisable shape. Here he first became involved in civic affairs, began to write, and revealed his talent for agitation. In the 1790s he reminded the town's citizens that many would recollect, '[W]hilst I resided among you, there was not a man more firm and open in supporting the principles of liberty than myself.'[3]

Lewes had been a centre of Republicanism in the English Civil War and a local Member of Parliament had signed Charles I's death warrant in 1649. Political opposition to the area's landowning family, the Pelhams, was concentrated among radical Whigs, who strove to maintain rather than overthrow the 'balanced' constitution of King, Lords and Commons. While Paine shared their view and was active in their cause, a surviving undercurrent of Republicanism in Lewes undoubtedly influenced him, as his later writings were to show.

Paine took lodgings in Bull House, where Samuel and Esther Ollive ran a tobacco and grocery business. Samuel Ollive had been a constable, an office equivalent to mayor, and remained closely involved in Lewes politics through his membership of the Society of Twelve, a self-recruiting clique of town worthies. Paine clearly impressed Ollive with his opinions and his ability to express them and it took his landlord little time to co-opt him into the Society of Twelve, drawing him into the body that undertook much of the town's administration. Here Paine gained experience in the day-to-day practice of local self-government. Paine, despite the revelation he had had as an eight-year-old, remained a Christian. He became a member of the Vestry, a church group, one of the functions of which was to act as a welfare body, collecting tithes to relieve local poverty. It was no doubt also at Ollive's urging that Paine became a member of the 'Headstrong Club', which held weekly meetings at the White Hart Hotel to eat, drink and debate political and social issues. Here Paine met Thomas 'Clio' Rickman (so-called because of his musical talent), who became a lifelong friend and, in 1819, a sympathetic biographer. In the club's stimulating atmosphere, Paine developed his ability to argue a case and won a reputation for eloquence. It was a tradition to award a prize at the end of the evening to the most persuasive speaker, something that Paine won regularly. A fellow member described Paine as a 'shrewd and sensible fellow' with a 'depth of political knowledge'.[4]

Paine may have met, and would certainly have admired, the radical politician John Wilkes, who was greeted in Lewes as a hero when he visited the town in August 1770. In 1762 and 1763 Wilkes had angered the established order with his newspaper the *North Briton*, in which he ridiculed George III and the government, denounced ministerial corruption and raised awkward questions about the rights of Englishmen. Paine would have known from his time in London of the popular movement for 'Wilkes and Liberty' and its strength among the artisans and shopkeepers to whom he would in the future direct his own radical message in two continents.

INGENIOUS YOUNG MAN

4

It was in Lewes that Paine began writing for a public audience, despite his later claims to the contrary. He was paid three guineas for producing a campaign song for a Whig Parliamentary candidate. He was also known to have written a long satirical poem, 'Farmer Short's Dog Porter: A Tale', based on the true story of the trial and execution of a dog whose owner had angered a powerful landowner by voting against his candidate. An elegy on the death of General James Wolfe (who had been killed capturing Quebec in the Seven Years War) published in Pennsylvania in 1775, but written in Lewes, suggested that Paine retained the patriotism that had taken him to sea against the French.

Paine's prowess as an ice skater earned him the nickname of 'the Commodore'. He was also a member of the bowls club, which met on the green below Lewes Castle. Here after a game Paine revealed a sympathy for Republicanism. Hearing a player say that he admired the King of Prussia because he 'had the devil in him', Paine commented that if that was a necessary quality for a monarch then '[K]ings might very well be dispensed with', a dangerous remark for a man whose livelihood demanded allegiance to George III.[1]

Paine's territory as an Excise officer extended to Brighthelmston (now Brighton), ten miles from Lewes. The area was rife with smuggling and the local newspaper reported regular and violent skirmishes between officers and smugglers. The Excise were as unpopular here with publicans and traders as in Paine's previous postings and the job remained poorly paid. As the officers turned to agitation for an improvement in their conditions, Paine would emerge as a leader, his political confidence growing and his awareness of the social and economic problems besetting England strengthened through his work and the Headstrong Club debates.

In 1769 Samuel Ollive died, leaving a wife, three daughters and a son. For reasons of propriety, Paine moved out of Bull House but was then invited by Esther Ollive to help run the shop, a conflict of interest for an Excise officer that apparently went unremarked. Paine's relationship with one daughter, Elizabeth, became closer and on 26 March 1771 they married in the Nonconformist Westgate Chapel, completing their vows, as the law demanded, in the Anglican church across the road. Paine, 12 years older than Elizabeth, declared himself a bachelor and made no reference to his previous marriage. The pattern of Paine's life with Mary was to repeat itself. After meeting the expenses of his post as an Excise officer, Paine was left with less than a pound a week. He had shown himself in Sandwich to be no businessman and the shop in Lewes, for which he was now responsible, ran into difficulties. Neighbours commented that Paine devoted more energy to politics and the accompanying socialising than to making a living, neglecting his wife in the process. Gossip also suggested there were sexual difficulties, either of incompatibility or impotence on Paine's part.

Paine was a little over a year into his marriage when he began to take a prominent part in the Excise officers' agitation. For Paine to be at the centre of a national campaign demonstrated the extent of his development in Lewes. In 1772 Paine's fellow officers turned to him to put their arguments in writing. He produced a 21-page pamphlet, *The Case of the Officers of Excise*, setting out the demands of what was, in effect, a trade union. One writer sees this as 'his first attempt at prose and his first defence of the underclass'.[2] Eight officers, including Paine, were signatories to the pamphlet, which was to be presented to the Commissioners of Excise, supported by a petition to Parliament.

Paine said in the pamphlet that the Excise provided the Crown with £5 million annually, while the men who raised this revenue were struggling to survive, part of 'the voice of general want' increasingly heard in England.

Some, he said, were tempted into corruption, not because this was inherent in human nature but because 'poverty and opportunity corrupt many an honest man'. Paine declared, 'Nothing tends towards a greater corruption of manners and principles than a too great distress of circumstances'. But Paine also made a broader point, one that questioned the organisation of English society itself, when he denounced 'the rich, in ease and affluence' whose wealth represented the 'misfortune of others'.[3]

Four thousand copies of the pamphlet and a petition signed by 3,000 Excise officers throughout the country were printed in Lewes for circulation among Members of Parliament and potential supporters. Shortly before Christmas 1772 Paine took leave from his post in Lewes to lobby Parliament, financed by what remained of contributions that each of the petition's signatories had made to the campaign. On 21 December Paine sent a copy of his pamphlet to the Irish writer Oliver Goldsmith, suggesting that they meet for a drink and conversation. Goldsmith agreed and the two met in London. Paine would have enjoyed some sympathy from Goldsmith, who had condemned in his poem 'The Deserted Village' a country in which 'wealth accumulates and men decay', and which Paine had echoed in the pamphlet.

The Commissioners rejected the Excise officers' demands out of hand and Parliament refused even to consider them. Paine, however, came under suspicion by some of the Commissioners as the author of a series of articles attacking corruption among magistrates, although there is no evidence that he wrote the offending pieces. After three months in London, Paine returned to Lewes. His problems over money were intensifying and his marriage, further undermined by prolonged separation, was failing.

It is remarkable that, given the conditions of 18th-century England, Paine should have been able to agitate against the Crown, which employed him, and to criticise the social order, and yet retain his liberty, let alone his office. However, the Board of Excise seized their opportunity when Paine's desperate financial straits provoked another absence. On 8 April 1774 the Board of Excise dismissed him by letter for having left his post without permission 'on account of debts he had contracted'. On 14 April Paine was declared bankrupt. The local newspaper advertised the sale by public auction of 'all the household furniture, stock in trade, and other effects of Thomas Pain, grocer and tobacconist'.

Finally, on 4 June 1774 the relationship between Paine and Elizabeth ended permanently. Paine remarked bitterly to a friend that the reason was '[N]obody's business but my own; I had cause for it, but I will name it to no one'.[4] A little over a year later, writing on the institution of marriage in general, Paine might have had his own partnership with Elizabeth in mind. 'Sure of each other by the nuptial band they no longer take any pains to be mutually agreeable; careless if they displease, and yet angry if reproached; with so little relish for each other's company anybody else's is welcome, and more entertaining. Their union thus broke, they pursue separate pleasures; never meet but to wrangle, or part but to find comfort in other society.'[5] Elizabeth died in 1808, a year before Paine.

Paine had no reason to remain in Lewes, the scene of his disappointment and humiliation, and travelled to London where he renewed his contact with former acquaintances, including Benjamin Franklin. Paine expressed an interest in going to North America. He was later to say that as a boy in Thetford he had read a history of Virginia and since that day thoughts of crossing the Atlantic had filled his mind. On 30 September Franklin wrote a letter of introduction addressed to his son William, then governor of New Jersey, and his son-in-law Richard Bache, a Philadelphia businessman. Franklin described Paine, who was now approaching 38, as 'an ingenious young man' with hopes of settling in Pennsylvania. He asked that they should 'give him your best advice and countenance, as he is quite a stranger there'. Franklin suggested that they helped Paine secure work as a clerk, school tutor or assistant surveyor 'so that he may procure a subsistence at least, until he can make acquaintance and obtain a knowledge of the country'.[6]

In October 1774 Paine abandoned England, sailing aboard the *London Packet*, captained by a friend from Lewes. In the Atlantic crossing all but seven of the 120 passengers on board, Paine included, became sick with 'ship fever', a form of typhus. Five died, Paine himself coming close to death. On 30 November he was carried ashore at Philadelphia and placed in the care of a doctor who had learnt from the ship's captain of Paine's close acquaintance with Franklin. After six week's convalescence he had recovered sufficiently to present his letter of introduction.

THE CLIMATE OF AMERICA

5

Paine arrived in the American colonies as a decade of campaigning against British authority was coming to a head. Britain had sought more effective control over the territorial gains in North America of the Seven Years War against France, in which Paine had participated as a crewman on a privateer. The war had been costly for Britain, with a doubling of the national debt. The government attempted to force the colonists to contribute through taxation towards the expense of maintaining 10,000 soldiers deployed to defend the western and Canadian frontiers. The colonists insisted their allegiance was to the King and that as they were not represented in Parliament, then Parliament had no right to legislate for them: 'No taxation without representation'. The British view was that the colonists, like the bulk of the disenfranchised population in the mother country, had a 'virtual' representation in Parliament.

The 13 colonies had been accustomed to a large measure of self-rule through their own Assemblies, with a governor in each colony representing the formal link with the Crown. The 1764 Sugar Act provoked resistance from New England merchants, who argued in a petition to the King that increased duties on imports threatened their trade with the Caribbean. There was resentment at the Quartering Act of 1765, which required the colonies to feed and accommodate British soldiers. Organised resistance by the 'Sons of Liberty', established by the representatives of nine colonies, forced the repeal of the 1765 Stamp Act, which had levied a duty on legal documents, newspapers and pamphlets. In 1766 the British attempted to re-assert Parliament's power to pass laws binding on the colonies with the Declaratory Act. A boycott of British goods following the passage in 1767 of the Townshead Duties, which imposed duties on the bulk of American imports, secured their repeal in 1770.

Events in Boston, in the colony of Massachusetts, showed the level the crisis had reached. What had begun in 1768 as little more than scuffles between British troops and protestors, culminated on 5 March 1770 in the 'Boston Massacre', in which five citizens were killed by musket fire. In 1773 the government passed the Tea Act, allowing the failing East India Company a monopoly on tea imports into the colonies. Boston voted to boycott the Company's imports and on 16 December protestors mounted the 'Boston Tea Party', throwing three shiploads of tea into the harbour. The British prime minister, Lord North, told the House of Commons, 'We are now to establish our authority, or give it up entirely.'[1] His government attempted to enforce control through what became known to the colonists as the Coercive (or Intolerable) Acts. Boston harbour was closed and the rights of the Massachusetts Assembly were curtailed. The commander of the British army in America, General Thomas Gage, was appointed governor of Massachusetts, with enlarged powers, including that of billeting troops in private homes.

The Coercive Acts provoked the colonists into a more thoroughly organised response and in September 1774, shortly before Paine's arrival, representatives of 12 of the colonies convened the First Continental Congress in Philadelphia. The Congress established a Continental Association to review British legislation affecting the colonies and to enforce a renewed boycott of goods from Britain and her Caribbean territories. The Congress called on the government to recognise their rights to represent and tax themselves. Local committees were formed throughout the colonies to supervise the boycott and persuade waverers, forms of organisation generating a popular politics extending beyond the traditional élites and laying the basis for what would grow into radical pressure for full democracy. If the colonists were unclear about the direction in which events were taking them, the King had no doubt. In November he told Lord North, '[B]lows must decide whether they are to be subject to the country or independent.'[2] But in the colonies, thoughts of independence were far from widespread. The majority of colonists saw themselves as Englishmen and limited their demands to what they saw as the rights of Englishmen. Nevertheless, the Continental Congress was prepared to defend those rights and advised the colonies to raise and arm militias.

Philadelphia, where Paine landed at the end of November 1774, was the unofficial capital of the American colonies. With a population of 30,000, Philadelphia had the largest port in the colonies and thrived on trade. Paine had arrived in a country in which, unlike the England he had fled, there were no hereditary titles and, it appeared, no privileges deriving solely from the accident of birth. Paine found a bracing egalitarianism in Philadelphia and would write two months after his arrival, 'There is a happy something in the climate of America … '.[3] What Paine's first impressions missed was the dominance in political life of the city's wealthier merchants, one that Philadelphia's artisans and labourers had only recently begun to challenge.

Early in January 1775 Paine visited Richard Bache to present his father-in-law's letter of recommendation. As Franklin had suggested, Bache secured Paine employment as a tutor and, having learnt of his interests, offered introductions to Philadelphia's spirited political life. Paine took a room in the centre of town, on the corner of Market and Front Streets, close to the slave market. Next door to his lodgings was a bookshop owned by Robert Aitken, a Scottish-born printer. On 10 January Paine entered the shop and, in the course of a conversation, impressed Aitken with the clarity of his political views and the breadth of his knowledge, and who then offered him the post of editor of a monthly magazine he was planning to set up with Dr John Witherspoon, the president of the College of New Jersey, *The Pennsylvania Magazine, or, American Monthly Museum*. Aitken proposed a £50 annual salary and advised Paine to avoid political or religious controversy.

Paine worked fast and the first edition of the *Pennsylvania Magazine* appeared on 24 January, two weeks after his appointment. The magazine's 52 pages included a biographical sketch of Voltaire, a digest of world events, book reviews, and a description of the working of an electricity generator. Paine had made a remarkable transition from dismissed Excise officer to journalist, one he later admitted had surprised him. He seized the opportunity the magazine offered to learn as he went, building on his debating experience in Lewes to develop a transparent and efficient style tempered to express the emerging politics. Paine's main audience would be people of his own background, artisans, self-educated, impatient with ornate language, anxious for the point to be made with a minimum of fuss, the words a preliminary to action. Witherspoon, the magazine's co-owner, with whom Paine came into conflict after sharply editing his contributions, was less impressed by Paine's personal style. He claimed that Paine could not write 'until he had quickened his thoughts with large draughts of rum and water'.[4] Whatever the truth of this, by the March edition subscriptions had climbed from an initial 600 to 1,500, giving the magazine the largest circulation of any similar publication in the colonies.

THUS FAR A QUAKER

6

Paine, with no real background as a journalist, was to contribute over 20 articles to the *Pennsylvania Magazine*, their range showing the virtuosity of his mind and his ability to turn his pen to any subject. Paine maintained the common practice of using a pseudonym for all his contributions. He produced two pieces for the magazine's first issue. One praised the magazine as a form for imparting information, while the second, 'To the Public', set out Paine's affection for his new homeland, under the pen name 'Atlanticus'. He compared the health of America favourably to that of Europe, which he saw as polluted.

In January Paine had written an imagined conversation between General James Wolfe (who had been killed in the capture of Quebec from the French in 1759) and General Gage (the British military commander enforcing the Coercive Acts) for a rival publication, the *Pennsylvania Journal*. The article demonstrated how quickly Paine had grasped the issues facing the colonists but also showed remaining illusions about the nature of the relationship with Britain. Gage argues in the dialogue that he is carrying out the orders of King George III as expressed through Parliament. Wolfe dismisses this, demanding Gage's resignation as the best means of restoring harmony between Britain and her colonies. Paine was later to write that he had seen the conflict as akin to a lawsuit, not a matter of war and independence.

In March Paine, again writing as 'Atlanticus', denounced the cruelties of British rule in India, an article that could easily be interpreted as a veiled criticism of Britain in America. In the same issue, under the pseudonym 'Justice and Humanity', he presented one of the most vigorous attacks on slavery hitherto written in the colonies. Paine said, 'That some desperate wretches should be willing to steal and enslave men by violence and murder for gain, is rather lamentable than strange. But that many civilized, nay, christianized people should approve, and be concerned in the savage practice, is surprising; and still persist, though it has been so often proved contrary to the light of nature, to every principle of Justice and Humanity, and even good policy, by a succession of eminent men …'. Paine asked his readers, 'With what consistency, or decency they complain so loudly of attempts to enslave them, while they hold so many hundred thousands in slavery; and annually enslave many thousands more, without any pretence of authority, or claim upon them?'.[1] He was to go further in October, looking to the day when America had gained its independence from Britain and the slaves their freedom from their white masters. Paine showed a wider and unexpected sympathy by adding his hope that even the American Indians would secure freedom from the white man's 'treachery and murder'.

On the eve of the American revolution a quarter of the population in the colonies, half a million people, were slaves. An estimated 78 per cent of exports were produced by slave labour. Though slavery as an institution predominated in the south, northerners were also involved in the slave trade. Virginia held the largest number, 200,000, 40 per cent of the colony's population. In the north, 14 per cent of New York's population were enslaved, 8 per cent of New Jersey's and 6 per cent of Rhode Island's. Pennsylvania was to introduce gradual abolition in 1780, Massachusetts in 1783, Rhode Island in 1784, and New York in 1785.

The March article on slavery attracted the attention of Benjamin Rush, a radical physician who had long held views similar to those Paine had expressed. The two became close friends. Rush introduced Paine to David Rittenhouse, an artisan-scientist, and to George Clymer, a prosperous merchant, both of whom were to play prominent parts in the independence struggle. Paine was becoming drawn into circles of friendship and shared opinion that would carry him to prominence. Shortly after the publication of the article, Franklin, who had now returned to the colonies, formed the first American anti-slavery body in Philadelphia, with Rush as president and Paine as a founding member.

In June Paine outlined proposals for a system of social security for the young and the elderly, a programme to which he would later return in more detail. With the experience of his own marriage as a guide, Paine's 'Reflections on Unhappy Marriages' contrasted the formality of European practice with what he said he had heard from an 'American savage'. For the American Indians there was no ceremony other than mutual affection and since relationships lasted 'no longer than they bestow mutual pleasures, we make it our business to oblige the heart we are afraid to lose; and being at liberty to separate, seldom or never feel the inclination'.[2] Once again, Paine could equally have been describing the relationship between Britain and her American colonies. Despite, or perhaps because of, his unhappy relationship with women, Paine showed himself to be an advanced thinker on the relationship between the sexes. 'Who does not feel for the tender sex?', he asked. 'Man with regard to them, in all climates, and in all ages, has been either an insensible husband or an oppressor ... Over three quarters of the globe Nature has placed them between contempt and misery.'[3] Despite this, Paine remained enough a prisoner of his time never to call for women to be given the vote.

Ignoring Aitken's advice to avoid controversy, Paine allowed the political struggle with Britain increasingly to dominate his writing, which took on a more focussed and committed tone as he felt his way towards the need for independence. British troops dispatched by General Gage to seize weapons held by the Massachusetts militia, the Minutemen, opened fire at Lexington on 19 April, killing eight and wounding ten. After destroying munitions in nearby Concord, the British marched back to Boston, harried all the way by the militia. Over 250 British soldiers were killed or wounded. Paine wrote, 'No man was a warmer wisher for a reconciliation than myself, before the fatal nineteenth of April, 1775, but the moment the event of that day was made known, I rejected the hardened, sullen-tempered Pharaoh of England ...'.[4]

Committees of Safety were formed from town to town, often comprising those excluded from traditional politics, such as artisans, small merchants and farmers. Paine quickly grasped the significance of this upsurge in popular feeling. On 15 May the Second Continental Congress, meeting again in Philadelphia, voted to formalise what was already an armed conflict with Britain, placing the colonial militias under the command of George Washington in a Continental Army. On 12 June General Gage imposed martial law and five days later British troops suffered heavy casualties dislodging

Americans from the fortified Bunker Hill in Boston. However, the majority of delegates to the Continental Congress remained reluctant to grasp the developing logic of the situation. In an 'Olive Branch Petition' Congress declared its loyalty to the King and asked for his help in securing reconciliation between Britain and the colonies.

Paine's response to these events was, first, to sting the British and their supporters with ridicule, and then, as his realisation of their meaning grew, to press the case for a decisive break. In May he criticised what he called the 'gothic and absurd' practice of duelling by aristocrats, an attack on the idea of aristocracy itself. In the same issue of the *Pennsylvania Magazine* he dismissed the concept of titles with contempt, implying his preference for a virtuous and egalitarian republic. 'When I reflect on the pompous titles bestowed on unworthy men', he wrote, 'I feel an indignity that instructs me to despise the absurdity'. He suggested that the King might well be called 'The Honorable plunderer of his country, or the Right Honorable murderer of mankind'. Titles, he declared, persuade people to 'admire in the great, the vices they would honestly condemn in themselves. This sacrifice of common sense is the certain badge which distinguishes slavery from freedom; for when men yield up the privilege of thinking, the last shadow of liberty quits the horizon'.[5]

In July Paine urged the need for physical force against Britain in his 'Thoughts on a Defensive War'. His primary argument was against the Quakers and the dilemma forced on them by their pacifism, one that his religious background allowed him to understand only too well. He had less sympathy for their view that only God could remove monarchs and governments. Quaker unwillingness to countenance violence against British forces led them to tacit support for those who wished to remain loyal to the Crown. 'Could the peaceable principle of the Quakers be universally established, arms and the art of war would be wholly extirpated.' But, he regretted, the world was not inhabited by angels. 'The peaceable part of mankind will be continually overrun by the vile and abandoned, while they neglect the means of self defense.' He compared Britain with the god Saturn, who had devoured his own children. Without the determination to resist, that would be America's fate. 'I am thus far a Quaker, that I would gladly agree with all the world to lay aside the use of arms, and settle matters by negotiation; but unless the whole will, the matter ends, and I take up my musket and thank heaven he has put it in my power.'[6]

The case for independence had yet to be made decisively, however. In August George III rejected the 'Olive Branch Petition', the attempt by the Continental Congress to secure a compromise, intensifying the crisis by declaring the colonies to be in a state of rebellion. Despite this apparent closing of any avenue to compromise, the Pennsylvania Assembly instructed its delegates to vote against independence if the matter was raised in the Continental Assembly. Paine reacted angrily, criticising the Pennsylvania Assembly, and other colonial assemblies that had taken a similar position, for overreaching their authority by treating the delegates as ciphers and issuing commands on a national issue of such importance.

Through the summer Paine had been drafting a pamphlet, which he intended to bring out under the title *Plain Truth*, presenting the arguments for the very act that the Pennsylvania Assembly and others were resisting. Paine had begun writing at Rush's suggestion. In late September he read the first complete draft at Rush's house to a small group of sympathisers. A dispute with Aitken, the joint owner of the *Pennsylvania Magazine*, ensured that Paine had the time to incorporate their comments. Aitken refused his request for an increase on the original £50 a year that had been agreed, and for a contract, and so Paine resigned at the end of November. In December Paine gave copies of what he intended to be the final draft of his pamphlet to Franklin, the man who had introduced him to America, to Rittenhouse, and to Samuel Adams, a brewer and prominent anti-British activist. Their comments were encouraging. By the end of 1775, hardly more than a year since Paine had first landed in the colonies, the pamphlet that would push the history of both America and Europe in a new direction was ready for the printer.

TO BEGIN THE WORLD OVER AGAIN

7

Clashes between the colonists and British forces had intensified while Paine was writing his pamphlet. In November 1775 American troops who had marched into Canada over the summer occupied Montreal. British soldiers burnt the town of Falmouth, while the Royal Navy bombarded Norfolk. The governor of Virginia, Lord Dunmore, urged slaves to rise against their owners, promising freedom to those who fought on Britain's side. The British government began deploying battalions of hired German troops alongside its own troops in the colonies.

Rush, who had first encouraged Paine to put his thoughts on paper, reminded him that the citizens of Philadelphia, like their counterparts throughout the colonies, remained reluctant to contemplate a break with Britain. He warned Paine above all to avoid two inflammatory words, 'independence' and 'republicanism'; both would be received unsympathetically and might put Paine's own life in danger with the British authorities. While Paine accepted Rush's suggestion for the pamphlet's title – *Common Sense* – he rejected the advice on content, producing a work that burnt with his passion for an American republic independent of Britain.

Acting on Rush's recommendation, Paine negotiated a contract with Robert Bell, a supporter of independence, to print, bind and distribute the pamphlet. Bell was to take half the profits, the rest to be paid into a fund to provide mittens for American soldiers in Canada. On 10 January 1776 *Common Sense; Addressed to the Inhabitants of America* appeared, a 50-page two-shilling pamphlet 'By an Englishman'. Popular opinion guessed that the writer was Rush, Franklin, John Adams or Thomas Jefferson, but not the obscure journalist Paine.

Though Paine hoped to influence the developing conflict, he could not have expected the intensity of his pamphlet's impact. He carefully constructed *Common Sense* to press two interlinked arguments on his readers. The first was to weaken any remaining faith the colonists had in Britain's 'balanced' constitution, which Paine denounced as both irrational and fraudulent. He used this to underpin his case for an independent, democratic and republican union. By setting out the inadequacy of the present order in vivid detail, he asserted the superiority of America's future. What had been militant protest by the colonists against British excesses was to be transformed into a national revolutionary overthrow of an alien despotism.

In his introduction Paine signalled to his readers the world-historical significance of the events they were living through: 'The cause of America is in great measure the cause of all mankind.' He then went on to make what was, for his time, a unique distinction between society and government. Men were in error, he said, if they confused them. 'Society is produced by our wants, and government by our wickedness; the former promotes our happiness positively by uniting our affections, the latter negatively by restraining our vices. The one encourages intercourse, the other creates distinctions. The first is a patron, the last a punisher.' Society, Paine argued, is a blessing, while government 'even in its best state is but a necessary evil ... the badge of lost innocence; the palaces of kings are built on the ruins of the bowers of paradise'. He drew his view of the efficacy of minimalist government (best when it governed least) from the principle in nature 'that the more simple anything is, the less liable it is to be disordered, and the easier repaired when disordered'.[1]

Paine then turned his attention to what he called 'the much boasted constitution of England'. He did not, as the radical Whigs had in Lewes, bemoan corruption of the constitution but condemned the constitution itself. He ridiculed the balance notionally existing between the King, Lords and Commons, asking how the Commons, whose role was to place a popular check upon the monarch, could then have their power checked by his rejection of their legislation. 'How came the King by a power which the people are afraid to trust, and are always obliged to check?' Certainly not from a wise people, nor, since the King's power required a check, could it have derived from God. Paine asked the source of the division of humanity into kings and subjects. He recognised the distinctions of male and female, which were of nature, and those of good and bad, but he could not understand 'how a race of men came into the world so exalted above the rest'. Writing for an audience he knew to be actively Christian, and who might take the view that there was a basis for monarchy in their religion, Paine challenged them to find any justification for such a belief in the scriptures. Where was the King of America? 'I'll tell you Friend, he reigns above, and doth not make havock of mankind like the Royal Brute of Britain.'[2]

Paine made anti-monarchism synonymous with republicanism, *res publica*, 'the public thing'. He accepted that Britain did not suffer under a despotic monarch as in, for example, Turkey. But this, he said, was to the credit of the English people, the Revolution of the 1640s and the beheading of Charles I. The execution had acted as a warning. Paine regretted, however, that while 'we have been wise enough to shut and lock a door against absolute Monarchy, we at the same time have been foolish enough to put the crown in possession of the key'.[3]

But to the evil of monarchy, Paine said, '[W]e have added that of hereditary succession; and as the first is a degradation and lessening of ourselves, so the second, claimed as a matter of right, is an insult and imposition on posterity'. And what, he asked, was the basis of George III's claim? William of Normandy's conquest of England in 1066. 'A French bastard landing with an armed banditti, and establishing himself as king of England against the consent of the natives, in plain terms a very paltry rascally original – it certainly hath no divinity in it.' In England, Paine said, the King was paid £800,000 a year to do hardly more than make war and grant offices. Monarchy had entered the world through violence and it was on war that monarchy thrived. 'Of more worth is one honest man to society, and in the sight of God, than all the crowned ruffians that ever lived.'[4]

Paine then moved to the American colonists' conflict with Britain. 'The sun never shined on a cause of greater worth', he wrote. This was no parochial affair but involved the fate of a continent, with effects that would last to the end of time. British troops had ended any possibility of reconciliation when they opened fire at Lexington. Britain did not hold her colonies for their protection, as many imagined, but to exploit them and drag them into war with her European rivals. Paine sneered at those who sought reconciliation.

'Hath your house been burnt?', he asked. 'Hath your property been destroyed before your face? Are your wife and children destitute of a bed to lie on, or bread to live on?' Even if some agreement were reached, Paine doubted the good nature of George III, 'an inveterate enemy to liberty'. Following any settlement, Paine asked, 'can there be any doubt but the whole power of the crown will be exerted, to keep this continent as low and humble as possible?'. Paine pointed to the geographical absurdity of the connection with Britain. 'To be always running three or four thousand miles with a tale or petition, waiting four or five months for an answer, which, when obtained, requires five or six more to explain it in, will in a few years be looked upon as folly and childishness.'[5]

But Paine was proposing more than a separation. He would later write, 'The independence of America, considered merely as a separation from England, would have been a matter but of little importance, had it not been accompanied by a revolution in the principles and practice of governments.'[6] He was urging a democratic revolution – 'to begin government at the right end' – but gave only what he said were 'hints not plans' of the form this new democracy would take. Paine had no doubt, however, that, 'A government of our own is our natural right'. He proposed the convening of a constitutional convention to frame a Charter of the United Colonies. The conference would be made up of 26 members of the Continental Congress, two representatives from each colonial Assembly, and five of the 'people at large', chosen by qualified voters in every one of the 13 colonies. The constitution would set out the number and manner of choosing members for a unicameral Congress, secure 'freedom and property to all men, and above all things the free exercise of religion, according to the dictates of conscience ... '.[7]

An independent America would live in friendship with Europe because it would be in the European interest to trade with her. 'The commerce by which she hath enriched herself are the necessaries of life, and will always have a market while eating is the custom of Europe.' Free from Britain, America would be free from entanglement in British conflicts. 'Every thing that is right or natural pleads for separation. The blood of the slain, the weeping voice of nature cries, 'TIS TIME TO PART.' Nothing, Paine wrote, 'could settle our affairs so expeditiously as an open and determined declaration for independence'.[8]

Paine issued a final call to arms, stirring the colonists with the message that implicit in their struggle was a mission to the peoples of the world. 'O ye that love mankind! Ye that dare oppose, not only the tyranny, but the tyrant, stand forth! Every spot of the old world is over-run with oppression. Freedom hath been hunted round the globe. Asia, and Africa, have long expelled her. Europe regards her like a stranger, and England hath given her warning to depart. O! receive the fugitive, and prepare in time an asylum for mankind.' And in an appendix to the pamphlet's second edition Paine urged the colonists to march into the future without fear: 'We have it in our power to begin the world over again ... The birth-day of a new world is at hand, and a race of men perhaps as numerous as all Europe contains, are to receive their portion of freedom from the events of a few months.'[9]

A STATUE OF GOLD

8

The first edition of *Common Sense* sold out in two weeks and the popular reaction was immediate and dramatic. Paine had shouted the word 'independence' out loud, mocked the monarchy, and dismissed the British constitution as a sham. In calling for a constitutional convention he had committed, in the eyes of the British government, the crime of sedition. The strengths of *Common Sense* lay in its timing and in its style. Paine's short pamphlet changed almost overnight the terms of the argument with Britain. He had placed before the American colonists the choice of surrendering what rights they had or striking out confidently for independence; there was no middle way.

Paine's triumph lay in pressing that choice at the very moment that circumstances were forcing a decision. The arguments Paine presented might be sophisticated, but his style was fresh and colloquial, flashing with images that were simple to grasp, stirring with a confidently righteous abuse of tyranny. Plain words from a plain man, the accumulated anger of the disappointment of his life in England transformed by the New World into a dazzling prayer to liberty. Paine would later say, 'It was the cause of America that made me an author'.[1] He wrote, as Rush had seen, common sense. Paine, uniquely, had taken what was already known by the educated – the ideas on rights and liberties set out in *The Second Treatise of Government* by the 17th-century political philosopher John Locke (although Paine said that he had never read Locke), together with classical republican principles – placed them clearly in a contemporary American context, and did so in a language that excluded no one. What Paine had to say was open to the inhabitants of America, whether artisans or craftsmen or members of the political and financial élites. But it was, above all, those who had been prominent in forming the Committees of Safety on the outbreak of fighting in April 1775 that he sought to influence, the rank and file of a revolution that he hoped would be national and democratic. Over a fifth of the three million colonists were estimated to have read the pamphlet or had it read to them.

An admiring reader wrote to the *Philadelphia Evening Post* asking who the author was and saying that he deserved 'a statue of gold'. At a church in Connecticut, *Common Sense* was read aloud from the pulpit as a sermon. A New England reviewer noted, 'We were blind, but on reading these enlightening words the scales have fallen from our eyes.' Washington, now commanding the Continental Army, commented on its likely effect on Congress, 'A few more of such flaming arguments as were exhibited at Falmouth and Norfolk, added to the sound doctrine and unanswerable reasoning contained in the pamphlet *Common Sense*, will not leave members at a loss to decide upon the propriety of separation.'[2] Paine felt no need for false modesty and was to write, 'The success it met with was beyond any thing since the invention of printing'.[3]

The future President John Adams, while the author's name was still unknown, showed some insight into Paine's character when he suggested to his wife that whoever had written the pamphlet had 'a better hand at pulling down than building'. There had been suggestions that Adams himself was the writer, which he denied on the grounds that he could never write with such 'strength and brevity'. He would later admit that 'without the pen of the author of *Common Sense*, the sword of Washington would have been raised in vain.'[4]

As with Aitken in 1775, Paine now argued with Bell, the publisher, over money. Bell demanded immediate payment for printing. Paine, who had already agreed that Bell should have half the profits, eventually paid £30 but turned to another publisher to produce a second longer and cheaper edition. Bell too printed a second edition. Numerous pirated editions were also circulating throughout the colonies and Paine estimated that within three months 120,000 copies were sold. As the wider significance of what Paine was saying about liberty and the rights of subjects was realised, *Common Sense* was translated, first into German and French, and editions were printed in Edinburgh, Berlin, Rotterdam, Copenhagen, Dubrovnik. His words found an echo as far east even as Moscow.

Paine's name finally appeared on a third edition in February 1776, confirming for all to see his ability to produce a work of genius, to shake the world about him. The man who had fled from England to America in 1774 to escape persistent failure, now revelled in his new-found success and recognition. There were stories that following the dramatic response to the first anonymous edition, Paine had been unable to resist revealing himself as the writer in Philadelphia's alehouses. But some hesitancy remained, despite his confidence that the time had come for the common people to seize the reins of power. He was to tell a Congressional committee in 1783, 'All the plans or prospects of private life (for I am not by nature fond of, or fitted for a public one and feel all occasions of it where I must act a burden), all these plans, I say, were immediately disconcerted, and I was at once involved in all the troubles of the country.'[5] Here, perhaps, is Paine's own explanation of why he felt more comfortable as an agitational writer, a catalyst for action, than as a politician engaged in the practicalities of power.

The publication of *Common Sense* opened a torrent of debate throughout the colonies as defenders and opponents praised and cursed Paine in newspapers and pamphlets. The radical circle in Philadelphia, of which Paine was now at the centre, came into the open, pressing his arguments for independence. Paine responded to attacks in 'Four Letters on Interesting Subjects', expressing his disappointment that candidates taking the radical position had failed in elections to the Quaker (and by default loyalist) dominated Pennsylvania Assembly. In an appendix to a new edition of *Common Sense* Paine accused the Quakers of mingling their religion with politics. He said that those who sought separation were seeking peace through an end to contention with Britain, but had been given no choice but to take up arms. 'We fight neither for revenge nor conquest; neither from pride nor passion; we are not insulting the world with our fleets and armies, nor ravaging the globe for plunder. Beneath the shade of our own vines are we attacked; in our own homes, and on our own lands, is the violence committed against us.' He suggested the Quakers preached to the British, 'for they likewise bear arms'.[6]

But even among those who shared Paine's desire for separation, there were concerns about the implications of his call for a sweepingly democratic republic. The democracy Paine implied was seen as a synonym for anarchy.

Adams, for example, wrote that he dreaded the effect that *Common Sense* might have on the people, by which he meant the common people. He did not have Paine's idealism, had no illusion that class conflict (something Paine seemed to ignore) would disappear in the new republic and feared for the interests of property in the face of a levelling democracy. In his *Thoughts on Government* Adams rejected Paine's unicameralism and advocated a two chamber legislature modelled on the British Parliament, a 'balanced' constitution in which the wealthy controlled the upper house and the ordinary citizens the lower. Adams criticised Paine personally as a newcomer to America and ridiculed his references to the Bible.

On reading the work, an angry Paine rushed to Adams's lodgings in Philadelphia and spent an evening arguing his case. Why, he asked, with no monarchy, no aristocracy and no established church would there be any need for a second chamber? With no hierarchy of wealth and power, America's democracy would be political and social, truly egalitarian. Adams, certainly more politically experienced than Paine, held his ground. Nevertheless, he wrote Paine a warm letter of introduction to General Charles Lee, an English immigrant living in New York. The two met and Lee wrote of Paine to Rush, 'His conversation has much life. He has genius in his eyes.'[7]

With the experience of the Pennsylvania Assembly in mind, Paine feared that the individual colonies would not summon up the courage to break with Britain, despite the fervour that *Common Sense* had roused in the streets. He accused the Assembly of deriving its power from 'our mortal enemy the King of Great Britain' and its members of acting as an obstacle in the way of independence. Paine placed his hopes in the Continental Congress. As Washington had prophesied, the pressure from below that Paine had encouraged galvanised the members. On 10 May Congress adopted a resolution calling for separation from Britain.

On 7 June, Richard Lee, a representative from Virginia, proposed that 'these United Colonies are, and of right ought to be, free and independent states'. Congress, with Paine prominent in lobbying members for support, gave a five-strong committee, including Franklin, Adams and Jefferson, the task of drafting a formal declaration. Less than two years after Paine's arrival in America, and less than six months after *Common Sense* had first appeared, America was casting aside its colonial childhood. America had been the making of Paine, and Paine could claim with some justification that he was making the United States.

THE AMERICAN CRISIS

9

On 4 July 1776, after a long and detailed debate, Congress approved Jefferson's draft of the Declaration of Independence, removing a criticism of the slave trade, for which Jefferson had blamed the King, because of the embarrassingly divisive issues it raised. These tensions were to fester until the Civil War in the 1860s, and beyond. Paine understood the colonies' diversity, one that went beyond the question of slavery, but perhaps underestimated, and certainly had to ignore in his journalism, the complex implications. He remained constant to his vision of one America, democratic, egalitarian and, above all, free from the constrictions of the Britain he had escaped.

There is no truth to the often-repeated story that Paine wrote the Declaration of Independence. Paine himself made no such claim. In 1805 he wrote to a correspondent, 'I was myself among the first that proposed independence and it was Mr Jefferson who drew up the declaration.'[1] But Paine and Jefferson, who maintained his friendship with Paine in the latter's darkest days, drank from the same well. Jefferson set out the colonists' objections to British rule and their right to govern themselves.

As in England, Paine's life in America was marked by almost continual poverty. On his resignation from the *Pennsylvania Magazine*, he lost £50 a year and his sporadic journalism yielded little. Selflessly generous, Paine had refused to accept a penny in payment for *Common Sense*, giving up, he calculated, as much as £1,000. In March 1776 political sympathisers had had to collect $100 to enable Paine to return from New York to Philadelphia and to pay for lodgings. With his consistent refusal to profit from his writings for the American cause, Paine would continue to depend for his very subsistence on the support of friends and allies, and, once independence had been won, the country's gratitude.

On 9 July the Declaration of Independence was read publicly to the citizens of Philadelphia, while Paine was already *en route* to Perth Amboy, New Jersey, as a volunteer in the 'Associators', a militia unit. From their encampment off the southern tip of Staten Island, where Paine stayed for two months, he watched the growing strength of the British forces, as ships unloaded troops and equipment. In May France had transported arms and ammunition to aid the American forces but Paine's own observations showed him how ill-equipped they were. On 12 July a further 30,000 British troops were deployed in New York, where General Washington had established his headquarters. Following an American defeat at the battle of Long Island in August, Washington withdrew across the Hudson River. In September, their term of enlistment having ended before they had seen action, the 'Associators' returned to Philadelphia. Paine moved to Fort Lee to act as unpaid aide to General Nathaniel Greene, who was, like Paine, a Quaker who had reluctantly accepted the need to take up arms. Paine dined each evening with the general's staff, gleaning information on the course of events and the state of the revolutionary forces. Paine used this intelligence in eyewitness reports for the Philadelphia press, acting, for the first time in history, as a propagandist journalist attempting to maintain civilian and military morale.

On 16 November Paine watched from high ground as the British under General Charles Cornwallis seized Fort Washington on Manhattan Island, opening the way to an advance on Philadelphia. Four days later Paine was part of a retreating army as General Greene abandoned Fort Lee in the face of 6,000 British and Hessian troops. Paine was to write a few months later, with a little bombast, of his own equanimity under cannon fire at the time. But a fellow militia member suggested that Paine, now almost 40 years old, lacked the military virtues. 'Paine may be a good philosopher,' he wrote, 'but he is not a soldier – he always kept out of danger.'[2]

With more volunteers drifting away, Washington's remaining forces retired to the west bank of the Delaware on 8 December 1776. Paine praised

Washington's conduct of the retreat, saying that God had 'given him a mind that can flourish even upon care'.[3] But despite the confident expectations of American strength he had set out in *Common Sense*, Paine was aware of the weakness of a citizen volunteer army with minimal training and little military discipline. His view, having observed the militia in action, was that they were the best troops in the world for a rapid engagement, but not for a long drawn-out campaign.

Paine returned to Philadelphia to find the Loyalists, or Tories as they were also known, who opposed independence, preparing to welcome General Howe and what they confidently expected to be his victorious army. There were an estimated 500,000 Loyalists opposing the revolution, 20 per cent of the white population, of which almost 20,000 fought for the British. They came from all classes, but predominated from the pre-war social and political élites. Some feared the economic effects of a break with Britain; others were concerned that violence would unleash chaos. At the end of the war 80,000 left the United States, many settling in Canada.

In a passion of desperation Paine wrote the first of a series of letters intended to rouse the faltering revolutionaries. Paine produced 16 papers under the title *The American Crisis* during the war, six of them in the critical years from 1776 to 1778. The first appeared in the *Pennsylvania Journal* on 19 December and within a few days 18,000 copies were printed as an eight-page pamphlet. As with *Common Sense*, Paine, determined that the price of the pamphlet should be kept as low as possible, asked for no payment. Thousands more copies were quickly brought out in pirate editions.

As Washington's army disintegrated and the cause of independence hung in the balance, Paine began what he had to say at a furious pace, condemning the faint hearts and making a virtue of the difficulties facing America. 'These are times that try men's souls. The summer soldier and the sun-shine patriot will, in this crisis, shrink from the service of their country: but he that stands it now, deserves the thanks of man and woman. Tyranny, like hell, is not easily conquered: yet we have this consolation with us, that the harder the conflict, the more glorious the triumph. What we obtain too cheap, we esteem too lightly: 'tis dearness only that gives every thing its value. Heaven knows how to set a proper price upon its goods; and it would be strange, indeed, if so celestial an article as freedom should not be highly rated.'[4]

Paine ridiculed the British commanders and denounced the Tories, their colonial supporters. 'Every Tory is a coward; for a servile, slavish, self-interested fear is the foundation of toryism; and a man under such influence, though he may be cruel, can never be brave.' He refused to 'make a whore of my soul, by swearing allegiance to one whose character is that of a sottish, stupid, stubborn, worthless, brutish man'. This was the George III to whom Paine had sworn loyalty when he had become an Excise officer. He criticised those who wanted only peace in their own time. He appealed to the colonists as parents. A generous parent would say, '[I]f there must be trouble, let it be in my days, that my child may have peace.' Paine drew attention to his own style as a writer to reinforce what he was saying. 'I dwell not upon the vapours of imagination, I bring reason to your ears; and in language as plain as A, B, C, hold up truth to your eyes.'[5]

Washington recognised the force of Paine's words, how they would appeal to the hearts and the minds of the army and the civilians behind the lines. Preparing to recross the Delaware and advance against the British, Washington ordered his officers to read the paper aloud to their men on Christmas Day 1776. That evening they crossed the river, surprised and routed the Hessians at Trenton, taking almost 1,000 prisoners. On 3 January 1777 the Continental Army pressed on to further success at Princeton.

Ten days later Paine published the second of *The American Crisis* series. For the first time he used the expression 'United States of America', which, he said, 'would sound as pompously in the world or in history as "the Kingdom of Great Britain"'.[6] (The word 'pompously' has altered its meaning since Paine's time.) Paine addressed the paper to Lord Howe, an admiral and brother of the British commander, and identified the fundamental weakness of the British in what was a war for national liberation. While certainly not equipped for military command, Paine showed an acute understanding of strategy, grasping the nature of wars that were to extend into the 20th century. 'Like a game of drafts, we can move out of one square to let you come in, in order that we may afterwards take two or three for one', he wrote. 'In all the wars in which you have formerly been concerned in you had only armies to contend with; in this case you have both an army and a country to combat.'[7] It would be easier, he said, for the Americans to start a revolution in England than for Britain to conquer America.

STRANGER WITHOUT CONNECTIONS

10

Although Paine's primary value to America was as an agitational writer, he was given a series of posts, partly to ensure him an income. In January 1777 he was appointed secretary to a commission negotiating treaties with the Indian tribes in Pennsylvania, with a one-off payment. His work began on 22 January and concluded successfully on 30 January, the day after his 40th birthday. However, Congress refused to ratify the treaties, to Paine's disappointment. He had written in the *Pennsylvania Magazine* two years earlier of his sympathy for the Indians and his hope that they would one day find their own freedom.

On his return to Philadelphia in February Paine was drawn again into local politics. Since September 1776 argument had been raging about the ultra-democratic Philadelphia Constitution, which had been drafted by Radicals and favoured the interests of artisans and small farmers. Paine suspected that its opponents, the Conservatives, were – as he had also suspected of Adams's attacks on *Common Sense* – more concerned to defend the interests of the colonial élite. Not that Paine wanted the rich excluded from their share in the nation. In response to charges that the Pennsylvania constitution was good for a poor man, Paine said he was not pleading the cause of one against the other. He was convinced that the true interest of one was the real interest of both. In March 1777 he was active in establishing a Whig Society, dominated by Radicals. Although Paine feared squabbling behind the lines in the midst of a fragile military situation, he argued in the *Pennsylvania Journal* in June that the constitution should remain and be tested in practice.

On 17 April Paine was appointed Secretary to the Committee of Foreign Affairs for Congress. Adams had recommended Paine for the post and the only objection had come from Dr Witherspoon, who remarked on Paine's drinking. The duties were largely routine, drafting correspondence to America's agents abroad and maintaining the Committee's records, the work of a civil servant rather than an architect of events. But Paine enjoyed the prestige (occasionally and inaccurately describing himself as Foreign Affairs Minister), the salary of $70 a month, and – as he told Franklin in a letter – the opportunity the post provided to gather information for a projected history of the American Revolution.

Two days after Paine's appointment, and on the second anniversary of the clashes between the Americans and the British at Lexington, he published a third edition of *The American Crisis*, an angry denunciation of the revolution's enemies. 'All we want to know in America is simply this', he wrote, 'who is for independence, and who is not?'. He proposed an oath of loyalty to the Declaration of Independence, with an extra property tax for those who refused. But those who went further and opposed the revolution should face 'the more rigid fate of the jail and the gibbet'.[1] This Jacobinism before its time was untypical of Paine and he could hardly have intended to be taken seriously. But given the military crisis, Paine could have been forgiven for alarm.

In July Paine wrote to Franklin (who had been representing American interests in Paris since 1776) that he and Rittenhouse were working on the production of a fire-tipped explosive arrow that could be shot into the British lines. On 11 September the British defeated the Americans at Brandywine Creek, forcing Congress to flee Philadelphia. Paine, writing dispatches to Franklin, had heard the gunfire of the battle and then the report of the defeat. He worked through the following night on a fourth edition of *The American Crisis*, taking it to the printers the next day. He had 4,000 copies produced at his own expense for free distribution. Paine's proposal to form a citizen's militia in Philadelphia and to barricade the streets was rejected by the Pennsylvania Assembly. As the British prepared to enter the city Paine fled, aware of the danger he faced of arrest.

After a further defeat at Germantown, the Continental Army retreated to Valley Forge, where Washington's men, demoralised and short of supplies, were to suffer a bitter and hungry winter. After his flight from Philadelphia, Paine went first to Washington's headquarters. He was dispatched from there to inspect the effectiveness of the American blockade of the Delaware. A fellow traveller reported on Paine's courage during a river crossing under British fire. On his return to Washington's headquarters the news came of victory on 7 October over British forces under General John Burgoyne at Saratoga. On 17 October Burgoyne surrendered his army.

Paine then went to stay in Bordentown with his friend Colonel Joseph Kirkbride, a Quaker who shared his suspicion of organised religion. Here he found a letter waiting him from the Pennsylvania Executive Council asking him to act as an intelligence officer supplying reports to the Assembly on the progress of the war. In November Paine conducted a four-day reconnaissance mission to secure information on British military intentions. On his return to Bordentown, Paine worked on plans to construct rocket-propelled boats to attack the British fleet blockading the Atlantic seaboard.

In the spring of 1778 Paine stayed first in York, where Congress was sitting, but there was little to occupy him as secretary to the Foreign Affairs Committee. On 13 February he moved into the home of William Henry, a scientist and gunsmith, with whom his friend Rittenhouse was also lodging. Paine amused himself with convivial discussions deep into the night, leading once again to accusations about his fondness for drink. One of Henry's sons was later to say that Paine ate a great deal and snored most of the day in an armchair. But Paine was also drafting the fifth of *The American Crisis* papers. The 24-page pamphlet was published on 21 March and sold, against Paine's wishes, at a cover price of 2s 6d.

The first part of Paine's paper attacked the British in the person of their naval commander, Lord Howe. 'Go home, sir, and endeavour to save the remains of your ruined country, by a just representation of the madness of her measures. A few moments, well applied, may yet preserve her from political destruction.' The second part concentrated on American morale and offered a practical proposal to reinvigorate the army. 'I would wish to revive something of that virtuous ambition which first called America into the field.'[2] Paine suggested drafting four men out of every hundred into service, with the remaining 96 supporting them with money and services. At a moment when Washington's abilities as a general were being questioned, Paine defended him.

The success at Saratoga had two beneficial effects for the American cause. In February the British Parliament proposed repealing the Tea Act and the Coercive Acts, removing its right to tax the colonies and, in effect, returning the relationship to what it had been in 1763. The British sent commissioners to negotiate, but Congress rejected any terms other than independence, confirming the struggle would continue. In the sixth edition of *The American Crisis* Paine questioned British wisdom in waging an unwinnable war and said that on their return to England the commissioners might 'carry back more Common Sense than they brought'. The second effect was on the French, who shared Paine's confidence in American victory. On 7 February America and France signed a Treaty of Amity and Commerce and a Treaty of Alliance. France recognised American independence and declared war on Britain in July. Fearing a French blockade, the British evacuated Philadelphia in June, enabling Congress and Paine to return to the city.

In November a confident Paine again taunted the British in a seventh edition of *The American Crisis*. He called on the manufacturing and mercantile population of Britain to rise against the King and the government, whom he accused of dragging the nation 'from madness to despair, and from despair to ruin. America has set you an example, and you may follow it and be free'. He said that his interests were not confined to America but were universal. 'My attachment is to all the world, and not to any particular part.'[3] But within months he had become embroiled in a controversy that threatened to undermine his reputation, forcing him from his position with Congress and threatening the place he had earned at the centre of the American cause.

In March 1776 a secret committee of Congress had delegated Silas Deane, a Connecticut lawyer and merchant, to conduct negotiations in France to secure weapons and supplies. He was to be paid expenses and a 5 per cent commission. In 1777 questions were raised about the extent of Deane's profits from the arrangement. He appeared to have claimed commission on a gift from the French government. Deane denied any wrongdoing, going public early in December 1778. Paine, as secretary of the Committee for Foreign Affairs, had charge of the papers dealing with the affair. From December 1778 to January 1779 he launched a series of attacks on Deane in the *Pennsylvania Packet* under the name 'Common Sense', extending the criticisms to others whom he believed had similarly benefited, including Robert Morris, a wealthy merchant and signatory of the Declaration of Independence. Paine's anger, and not only his, had been aroused by fears that the disinterested public-spiritedness essential for a truly democratic revolution had been undermined by the pursuit of personal profit.

Deane's supporters rallied, charging Paine with being a divisive enemy of the revolution for his willingness to attack a patriotic American. But Paine entered even more dangerous waters by revealing secret negotiations that America and France had been conducting, embarrassing both governments. Paine had sworn an oath of confidentiality on taking his office. He was denounced in the press as a 'stranger, without either connections or apparent property in this country'. On 7 January 1779 Paine admitted to a session of Congress that he was the author of the articles and resigned his post. Free from any responsibility, Paine, now writing as 'Comus', lashed out in print not only at Deane and Robert Morris, but also at Gouverneur Morris, who had scorned Paine's origins and his grammar when *Common Sense* appeared in 1776. Paine's suspicions about Deane's character were confirmed when it was revealed in 1781 that Deane was urging reunification with Britain.

NEITHER THE PLACE NOR THE PEOPLE

11

Paine was more affected by the Deane affair and what had followed than he would later admit. In the 1790s he wrote of the aftermath, 'As my object was not myself, I set out with the determination, and happily with the disposition, of not being moved by praise or censure, friendship or calumny, nor of being drawn from my purpose by any personal altercation; and the man who cannot do this, is not fit for a public character.'[1] But Paine showed greater honesty about his feelings to his friend Franklin, acknowledging in March 1779 that he had fallen from 'high credit to disgrace'.

Paine was abused in the streets of Philadelphia and attacked physically on at least one occasion. He virtually withdrew from public life as his character was vilified. One critic turned to verse in the *Pennsylvania Evening Post*, 'Go home, thou scoundrel, to thy native soil, And in a garret, labour, starve, and toil.'[2] But Paine retained his friends among the Radicals. In July several thousand supporters at a town meeting declared Paine to be a friend to the American cause and vowed to defend him as long as that remained the case.

Owen Biddle, another radical and a friend since 1776 who was now head of the Pennsylvania Board of War, ended Paine's isolation, offering him a temporary post as a clerk in April. The duties were once again mundane, particularly so for a man whose words had echoed across the world. Paine's low salary covered little more than rent and food. He complained to a friend that he could not even afford to hire a horse. He later told Washington that he had found the need to accept the post humiliating and had tried to keep it secret for fear that the world, knowing the contribution Paine had made to independence, would see in his plight a lack of generosity on America's part. But Paine's poverty intensified his awareness of the inflation gripping the states and the desperate plight of the poorest of the new country's citizens. The Deane affair had thrust into prominence the divisions of class and wealth that remained beneath the surface of the struggle for independence. It was to these that Paine now returned.

In January 1779 Paine might have seen sailors armed with clubs marching through Philadelphia to press their case for higher wages. In May he would certainly have seen a company of militia present a petition to the Pennsylvania Assembly protesting at the suffering of the 'middling and poor'. In one month alone prices had risen by 45 per cent. The causes were mixed: the effect of war and the weakness of a Continental paper dollar circulating simultaneously with state currencies. But there was a popular view in Philadelphia that Tories, merchants and the wealthy were forcing prices up through speculation. *Ad hoc* committees were already attempting to stem the rises through a combination of appeals to better nature and intimidation. Though no leveller or enemy of the rich, Paine had questioned their position in the *Pennsylvania Packet* in January. He argued that labour not property was the source of wealth, and that where there were none to labour, land and property were not riches.

As the son of a small trader and as someone who had tried his own hand at business, however unsuccessfully, Paine accepted the workings of the market, but in the face of the suffering caused by rising prices believed there was a wider social need for control through government and voluntary action. Paine found the contradiction difficult to surmount. On 27 May 1779 he was elected with Rittenhouse and other radical associates to a committee charged with investigating sales of flour by Robert Morris, with whom Paine had clashed in the Deane affair. Morris was exonerated and he and Paine would go on to develop an unexpected mutual respect. On 2 August Paine was placed on a committee to regulate salt and flour prices and another to raise taxes in Pennsylvania to help curb the inflation. Paine now found himself criticised by his old friend Rush, who declared that democracy was degenerating into mobocracy.

Observing the ineffectiveness of price controls in practice drew Paine closer to a *laissez-faire* view of the economy. As those who had opposed controls had argued, the result had been that salt and flour disappeared from the market. It would be some time before Paine could summon an equation that might enable a government to be minimal but interventionist, that could encourage a free market but at the same work for equality.

Paine continued to attract criticism, partly as a result of his role in the campaign. One newspaper condemned him as a 'disturber of the peace, a spreader of falsehoods, and sower of dissension among the people'.[3] In August, weakened by poverty and the stress he had endured since the Deane affair, Paine succumbed to a fever that confined him to bed for several weeks. Dispirited, the 42-year-old Paine wrote to one friend that unless he altered his way of life, '[M]y way of life will alter me'. Paine suggested to Franklin that he might visit France. And to a third friend he revealed a weakness of commitment to America that would have confirmed the prejudices of his enemies. Aware of the low esteem in which he was held by some, Paine wrote to Henry Laurens, '[P]erhaps America would feel the less obligation to me did she know, that it was neither the place nor the people but the Cause itself that irresistibly engaged me in its support; for I should have acted the same part in any other country could the same circumstances have arisen there which have happened here.'[4]

Once his sickness had passed, Paine turned his attention to raising money from the only source available, his writings. He wrote to the Pennsylvania Assembly's Executive Council seeking a £1,500 loan to enable him to publish his collected works. Paine was confident that sales would enable him to repay this sum in a year. The Council rejected his request but in October 1779, as the radical Constitutionalists won control in elections, offered him the post of clerk to the Pennsylvania Assembly. Paine began work taking minutes and drafting committee reports on 2 November, cheered both by the salary and the support the appointment showed he had in the Assembly.

Apparently reinvigorated, Paine published a further edition of *The American Crisis* on 26 February 1780, a spirited address 'to the people of England' intended to boost American morale in the midst of continuing military crisis, despite France, Spain and then Holland having been drawn into war against Britain. Paine had read aloud to the Pennsylvania Assembly a dispatch from Washington describing the hardships his men had suffered over the winter for lack of supplies. With the Continental Army on the edge of mutiny, Paine warned the British that they could expect the war to be brought home to them following the successes of the American naval commander and friend of Paine's, John Paul Jones.

In 1775 Paine had set out his abhorrence of slavery in the *Pennsylvania Magazine* and had linked hopes of liberty for America with the institution's abolition. On the day that Paine had taken up his post as clerk, the radical George Bryan had introduced a bill to free slaves in Pennsylvania when they reached the age of 21. At Bryan's request, Paine drafted the preamble to legislation that was opposed by the owners of the state's 6,000 slaves and merchants involved in the slave trade. Paine neatly entwined two forms of captivity when he wrote, 'We esteem it a peculiar blessing granted to us, that we are enabled this day to add one more step to universal civilization, by removing, as much as possible, the sorrows of those, who have lived in undeserved bondage, and from which, by the assumed authority of the King of Great Britain, no effectual, legal relief could be obtained.'[5] Compromises had, however, been necessary. In the legislation the Assembly passed on 1 March 1780 only the children of slaves were to be freed, and then not until they were 28. Paine was sorely disappointed at the watering-down of his original hopes and a decade later would write that he despaired of ever seeing an end to the trade in human beings.

On 12 May the British forces, which had been advancing through the southern states, captured Charleston, taking over 5,000 prisoners, the worst American defeat of the war. Paine issued a ninth edition of *The American Crisis*, declaring that 'America ever is what she thinks herself to be.' Unlike Britain, Paine wrote, '[T]he cause of America stands not on the will of a few but on the broad foundation of property and popularity.'[6] But more practically, Paine called on the wealthy to contribute to a fund to support the troops. He donated 500 Continental dollars and promised more. Robert Morris followed Paine with a substantial contribution. The plan then broadened into establishing a bank. Morris and others subscribed significant amounts until £300,000 in hard rather than Continental currency had been raised. Congress pledged to underwrite what became the Bank of Pennsylvania, returning Paine's original $500 on the grounds that his poverty was well known.

NEVER WAS A MAN LESS BELOVED

12

The award of an honorary Master of Arts degree at the University of Pennsylvania's first graduation ceremony on 4 July 1780 showed there had been some restoration in Paine's standing. But the satisfaction this brought was temporary and by the autumn Paine was again contemplating leaving America, hoping to repeat the success of *Common Sense* on new terrain. His plan, which he communicated to General Greene (to whom Paine had acted as aide in 1776), was to enter England in disguise and publish a pamphlet that would 'open the eyes of the country with respect to the madness and stupidity of the government'. Paine suggested a novel method of financing his mission. 'Drop a delegate in Congress at the next election, and apply the pay to defray what I have proposed; and the point then will be, whether you can possibly put any man into Congress who could render as much service in that station as in the one I have pointed out.'[1] Greene was able to convince him of the danger of the enterprise.

In *The Crisis Extraordinary*, published in October 1780 at his own expense, Paine returned to the need to raise taxes to pursue the war. He accepted that tax was a gift from citizens to their government but urged that Congress be granted powers of direct taxation rather than having to work through the states, as the Articles of Confederation insisted. (The Articles of Confederation and Perpetual Union were adopted by the Continental Congress on 15 November 1777 but not ratified by every state until 1 March 1781. The Articles, which were in effect little more than a military treaty, created a loose confederacy granting Congress limited powers to raise money and an army from the 13 states, to engage in diplomatic relations with other nations, and to settle inter-state disputes. Authority was exercised by Congressional committees rather than a central executive.) To those who objected to his taxation proposals, Paine argued that it would cost less to win the war, 13s 4d per head of the American population, than it would to lose it. After victory, he said, the government's need for revenue would fall to 5s per head; under British rule the population would have to pay £2.

Ten dozen copies of the pamphlet were distributed to the Pennsylvania Assembly, which went on to accept a call from Congress for higher taxes. In a further pamphlet in December 1780, *Public Good*, Paine called for the Articles to be replaced by a constitution that would establish strong central government. The constitution would be agreed by a popularly-elected national convention. Criticising Virginia's claim to western lands, which Paine argued should be held for the states in common, he appealed to the states to recognise that they were the United States and to co-operate in the interest of the nation as a whole.

By the time *Public Good* appeared, Paine was preparing to sail for France. In October, the Radicals having lost control of the Pennsylvania Assembly, he resigned his post as clerk. His first intention was to set up a newspaper and he had already begun buying stocks of paper. But on 22 November 1780 Congress approved a proposal to seek a loan from France. Colonel John Laurens, the son of Paine's friend Henry Laurens, was offered the mission to Paris to negotiate terms. Before accepting, Laurens, one of Washington's staff officers, discussed the suggestion with Paine who, still keen to leave America, was either invited to accompany Laurens or invited himself.

It was through Laurens that Paine now met the Marquis de Chastellux, a major general and member of the French Academy, who had pressed Laurens for an introduction to the author of the 'excellent work' *Common Sense*. Chastellux's diary entry for 14 December is a vivid and perceptive description of Paine's way of life and character. 'I discovered, at his apartments, all the attributes of a man of letters; a room pretty much in disorder, dusty furniture, and a large table covered with books lying open, and manuscripts begun.' Chastellux went on, 'His person was in correspondent dress, nor did his physiognomy belie the spirit that reigns throughout his works.' And, more tellingly, the Marquis recognised that Paine was no politician. 'As his patriotism and his talents are unquestionable, it is natural to conclude that the vivacity of his imagination and the independence of his character, render him more calculated for reasoning on affairs, than for conditioning them.'[2] On the same day, Paine met the Marquis de Lafayette, who was to become a close friend.

Gilbert du Montier, Marquis de Lafayette, was born in Auvergne, France, and joined the army at the age of 16. In 1777 he volunteered to support the American independence struggle for no pay, serving as a major general with Washington and seeing action at Brandywine (where he was wounded) and Yorktown. On his return to France, Lafayette supported the 1789 Revolution and commanded the National Guard, but fled following accusations of monarchist sympathies. In 1815 he re-entered French politics and in 1830 led the revolution that deposed the restored Bourbon monarchy.

There were objections in Congress to the proposal that Paine should accompany Laurens to France as an official emissary, with his old adversary Dr Witherspoon prominent in the attacks. Although he was ultimately to be proved right in his view of Deane, the controversy had raised questions about Paine's judgement and his discretion in matters of state. But, had Paine known it, the cruellest cut came from Franklin's daughter, Sarah Bache, with whom Paine had a close acquaintance. She wrote to her father from Philadelphia on 14 January 1781, 'There never was a man less beloved in a place than Paine is in this, having at different times disputed with everybody. The most rational thing he could have done would have been to have died the instant he had finished his *Common Sense*, for he never again will have it in his power to leave the world with so much credit.'[3]

On 19 January Paine failed to be shortlisted for membership of the American Philosophical Society following a discussion in which he had been the object of criticism, not least for his truculent personality. Paine, as clerk to the Pennsylvania Assembly, had signed the legislation incorporating the Society. The rejection, and the attitude of some Congress members, stung. Paine told Laurens that he would accompany him to France as a private citizen, paying his own way. Paine sold his few possessions, cleared his debts, and on 11 February, after a meeting with Washington, sailed from Boston on the gunboat *Alliance* with Laurens and his secretary. He had just turned 44. The Atlantic voyage was a risk for Paine, who had more to fear from capture by the British than his companions. But after a relatively uneventful voyage, the ship docked at L'Orient on 9 March. Paine was delighted to discover from the welcome he received that his name was almost as well known in

France as in America. The party then moved to Nantes, where a Philadelphian, Elkanah Watson, with whom Paine stayed, noted unflatteringly in his diary that Paine was 'coarse and uncouth in his manners, loathsome in his appearance, and a disgusting egotist.' Watson added that Paine spoke incessantly, 'rejoicing most in talking of himself and reading the allusions of his mind' and that he had had to persuade Paine, who had been at sea for three weeks, to take a bath because of his 'brimstone' odour.[4]

Paine travelled on to Paris, where he stayed near Franklin's home in the suburb of Passy. Speaking no French, Paine was unable to play any direct part in the negotiations. However, his clear tones were evident in Laurens's report to Congress and during the course of the mission Paine compiled memoranda and notes on America's military and financial plight. France agreed to make a grant of six million livres, a loan of ten million and to provide 20,000 uniforms, arms and other equipment. At the end of May a ship left for America carrying Lafayette and the much-needed supplies. On 1 June Paine and Laurens left Brest on a French frigate carrying two and a half million livres in silver. The crossing to Boston took 86 days, as the ship evaded British naval patrols.

While Laurens was paid $200, Paine received no reward and no credit for his part in a mission that had strengthened the American forces in material and morale. On 17 October General Cornwallis, surrounded at Yorktown, surrendered, sapping the British will to fight on (the prime minister, Lord North, wrote in his diary, 'Oh God! It's all over') and opening the way to peace negotiations. On 30 November, seven years to the day since he had arrived in Philadelphia, Paine's disappointment at his treatment erupted in a letter to Washington. Paine said he had always determined never to profit from his writings for the cause of independence, but he had hoped that America would have dealt as generously and honourably with him as he had dealt with America. He described the poverty he had endured and how, now the struggle was almost won, all he met were concerned at the neglect he had suffered but could offer no reason. He felt he had no alternative but to leave, to go to France or Holland. 'I have literary fame, and I am sure I cannot experience worse fortune than I have here.' He found it 'peculiarly hard that the country which ought to have been to me a home has scarcely afforded me an asylum'.[5]

At Washington's suggestion, Paine, after discussions with Robert Morris (now Superintendent of Finances) and Secretary for Foreign Affairs Robert Livingston, was offered the post of paid propagandist for Congress at an annual salary of $800. The agreement drawn up on 10 February 1782 specified that Paine should be paid from the secret services fund and that the matter should remain private so as not to 'injure the effect of Mr Paine's publications, and subject him to injurious personal reflections'. In 1779 Paine had dismissed a similar offer from the French ambassador on the grounds that an author who wrote for money was no better than a prostitute who sold her body.

A GREAT NATION

13

Paine's career as a 'mercenary writer' lasted less than a year. With Morris's resignation as Superintendent of Finances early in 1783, the payments ended. Paine had avoided possible embarrassment by stipulating that he should write nothing he disagreed with. Sharing the views of Morris and those around him on the need for strong central government made the task easier. A collapse of the authority of Congress as the war was ending would mean an end to his vision of the United States of America. Paine's views separated him from many of his radical associates, raising difficult questions about the balance between an essentially locally-based democracy, which he had begun by championing, and national government. Paine attempted to strike a balance by arguing that every citizen had two 'personalities', a local one and a national one, and that each supported the other.

Paine's first contribution as a propagandist had been a tenth edition of *The American Crisis* in March 1782, in which he described tax as an insurance. In an article for the *Pennsylvania Journal* in April he wrote that taxation was necessary to 'protect the aged and the infant, and to give liberty a land to live in'. Meetings with Washington, Morris and Livingston to discuss Paine's subjects flattered his sense that he had been restored to a place at the centre of events. On 17 March Paine invited Washington to 'spend part of an evening at my apartments, and eat a few oysters or a crust or bread and cheese'.[1] He said that he wished to talk over important public business with him and Morris. Washington certainly had some affection for Paine, as events were to show. Morris had less, but he respected Paine's abilities with the pen.

Paine's restoration was marked by his invitation, with a thousand other members of the political, military and social élites, to a banquet at the French Embassy in July celebrating the birth of a son to Louis XVI. Paine was ill at ease in the pomp and luxury, refusing to dance and reluctant to speak. Rush, who had encouraged him in 1776 to write *Common Sense*, noted in his diary that Paine appeared a 'solitary character', retiring to the garden 'to analyze his thoughts and to enjoy the repast of his own mind'.[2] With some relief, Paine left Philadelphia to spend the summer at Bordentown with his friends the Kirkbrides.

Ostensibly drafting his long-projected history of the American struggle, Paine instead wrote a closely-argued critique of a recent study of the revolution by a radical French theologian, Abbé Guillaume Raynal. Seeking to explain the American revolution to Europe, Paine disputed two points Raynal had made – that the colonists' revolt had been triggered by a reluctance to pay taxes, and that America had rejected Britain's offer of peace in 1778 because of the alliance with France. In his *Letter to the Abbé Raynal, on the Affairs of North America* Paine said that the rejection had preceded the alliance. But more fundamentally he denied that the revolution had had so narrow a cause. The colonists had risen to support the eternal principles of democracy. 'The true idea of a great nation is that which extends and promotes the principles of universal society; whose mind rises above the atmosphere or local thoughts, and considers mankind, of whatever nation or profession they may be, the work of one Creator.'[3] The pamphlet, published at Paine's own expense in September 1782, was favourably received in America and France, where he was already well known. The French government gave him a grant of 50 guineas, and possibly a further 2,400 livres for his services in writing articles reminding the Americans what they gained from the alliance. Pirated editions in London and Dublin renewed the fame Paine had achieved six years earlier with *Common Sense*.

Paine's main task was to use his talent to press the case for a 5 per cent import tariff that Congress had been attempting to impose since 1781. Rhode Island had refused to ratify the levy, accusing Morris of using the tariff to impose a centralised government. From December 1782 to February 1783 Paine wrote a series of public letters to persuade the Rhode Island Assembly to relent. He did not deny that the ultimate objective was a strong central government. The union, he wrote, was 'our Magna Carta – our anchor in the world of empires ... It is on our undivided sovereignty that our greatness and safety, and the security of our foreign commerce, rest'.[4] He visited Rhode Island to reinforce his message but was accused of being a mercenary employed by Congress to interfere in the state's affairs. Paine refuted the charge vigorously and, strictly speaking, dishonestly.

On 18 April 1783 Washington declared hostilities with Britain at an end. The following day, on the anniversary of Lexington, Paine composed the 13th edition of *The American Crisis*. Echoing the first edition, Paine wrote, 'The times that tried men's souls are over – and the greatest and completest revolution the world ever knew, gloriously and happily accomplished.' It was, he said, in America's power to 'make the world happy – to teach mankind the art of being so – to exhibit, on the theatre of the universe a character hitherto unknown – and to have, as it were, a new creation entrusted to our hands, are honors that command reflection, and can neither be too highly estimated, nor too gratefully received'. But he warned the new country that 'a fair national reputation is of as much importance as independence. That it possesses a charm that wins upon the world, and makes even enemies civil. That it gives a dignity which is often superior to power, and commands reverence where pomp and splendor fail'. Paine declared that he would 'always feel an honest pride at the part I have taken and acted, and a gratitude to nature and providence for putting it in my power to be of some use to mankind'.[5]

For Paine the war's conclusion threatened the collapse of the identity he had so skilfully constructed in 1776 – the author of America's revolution. The fates of Paine and America were intertwined, but with the latter's triumph, Paine, now 46, feared a return to the desperation that had driven him from England. In May 1783 he had to give up his lodgings in Philadelphia and stay first with the Kirkbrides and then with Owen Biddle. Paine now began the humiliating process of begging America to make some provision for him. On 7 June he wrote to Congress that he had no estate or fortune to support him and that, in the past, he had 'neither sought, received, nor stipulated for any honors, advantages, or emoluments for myself'. A fortnight later he complained to a Congressional committee that he had 'the honor of being ranked among the founders of an empire, which does not afford me a home'.[6] In September Washington advised him to go to Congress personally, believing Paine's presence might remind the members of his services to the country.

Paine was unable to attend a grand dinner celebrating news of the Treaty of Paris, signed on 3 September 1783, which brought the war with Great Britain to an end, as he was confined to bed for a month with scarlet fever. But in November he accepted Washington's invitation to stay at his new home near Princeton, Rocky Hill, a gift from Congress. Here they indulged their interests in scientific experimentation, testing the chemical composition of a nearby creek by setting fire to it. On 25 November, as the last British troops embarked from New York, Washington and Paine rode together at the head of a joyful parade.

In the autumn Paine had bought a house and a small patch of land close by the Kirkbrides' home in Bordentown. But Paine soon tired of country life and returned to Philadelphia where he published the final edition of *The American Crisis* on 9 December. He again pressed the need for a strong United States, one nation rather than 13 squabbling countries. 'United, she is formidable ... separated, she is a medley of individual nothings, subject to the sport of foreign nations.'[7]

On 12 June 1784 Washington wrote to his fellow Virginia Assembly member James Madison, 'Can nothing be done in our Assembly for poor Paine? Must the merits and services of *Common Sense* continue to glide down the stream of time, unrewarded by this country?' The Assembly, which recalled Paine's opposition to their claim to western lands, refused. But five days later New York presented Paine with a house and 270 acres at New Rochelle, the confiscated property of a Loyalist. Paine made it plain he would have preferred straight cash. He told Washington the gift was worth 1,000 guineas but he could not sell it for fear of appearing ungrateful. Instead, Paine rented it out to secure an income. On 26 August Congress finally resolved to acknowledge his contributions 'in explaining and enforcing the principles of the late revolution by ingenious and timely publications upon the nature of liberty, and civil government'.[8] Congress paid $3,000 on 3 October, sufficient (with a further $500 donated by the Pennsylvania Assembly) to keep Paine from hardship for the next two decades.

Paine's final involvement in American politics came in a controversy over the Bank of North America, which had grown from his original $500 subscription of 1780. The Bank had begun operating under a charter from Congress and the Pennsylvania Assembly in 1782. In 1785 the Assembly threatened to revoke the charter, following the Bank's refusal to accept a new paper currency the Assembly had issued. Paine distrusted paper currency, which he connected with the Continental dollar and inflation, and in the argument found himself against his old Constitutionalist allies. The Assembly voted to rescind the Bank's charter in September 1785. Paine responded in February 1786 with *Dissertations on Government; the Affairs of the Bank; and Paper Money*, hoping, unsuccessfully, to influence a debate on a motion to restore the charter. But the affair also caused Paine to question the Pennsylvania Constitution that he had defended in 1778. Formerly an advocate of an annually elected unicameral legislature, Paine confounded his radical associates by expressing what had traditionally been the conservative preference for two chambers. Tyranny could as easily take root in a single chamber dominated by one party as in any aristocracy.

BRIDGES AND CANDLES

14

In September 1785 Paine received a letter from his parents in Thetford, the first since 1775. For most of the year he had been living in New York, renting out his properties in Bordentown and New Rochelle, and much in demand. He dined regularly with the families of Commodore James Nicholson, who had fought in the Continental Navy, and General George Clinton. One commentator described Paine as 'a fashionable member of society, admired and courted as the greatest literary genius of his day'.[1] But in the autumn Paine, financially secure for the first time in his life, retired to Bordentown to follow what he now described as his real interest, 'the quiet field of science'.[2]

Paine's patron Benjamin Franklin had recently returned from France and in September Paine wrote a letter of welcome. Franklin replied that Paine should be in Philadelphia, where his abilities were missed, but understood that he was engaged in an 'arduous undertaking'. Paine had two projects in hand, designing an iron bridge and producing a smokeless candle. On 31 December Paine sent a parcel of the candles to Franklin, with a detailed description of their working. 'I do not, Dear Sir,' Paine wrote, 'offer these reasons to you but to myself, for I have often observed that by lending words to my thoughts I understand my thoughts the better'.[3] The following day Franklin and Paine dined together, experimenting with the candles after their meal.

Paine then became entangled in the Bank of North America affair, putting aside his bridge design and abandoning any thoughts he might have had of marketing the candles. But by May 1786 he was free to resume his work, aided by John Hall, an English mechanic who had recently moved to Bordentown, and a team of assistants. Paine later said that the idea for the bridge, which was to be without piers to cope with ice on American rivers, had come to him when observing a spider's web. On 6 June he dispatched Hall to Franklin with two models, one of wood and one of cast iron to display in his garden. In November Paine learnt that the Pennsylvania Agricultural Society was seeking rights from the Assembly to construct a bridge across the Schuylkill River. Working hurriedly, Paine and Hall completed a wrought-iron model by 26 December, which they showed to Franklin and Paine's old friend and fellow enthusiast Rittenhouse. Both encouraged Paine to petition the Assembly for a subsidy, though Rittenhouse doubted the American iron industry was capable of meeting Paine's demands. On 1 January 1787 Paine exhibited his work in the Pennsylvania State House courtyard. As one committee and then another considered the proposal, he despaired. Franklin suggested endorsements from the Royal Society in London and the Academy of Sciences in Paris might encourage an investor.

On 31 March Paine told Franklin that he planned to go to France to promote his bridge and then on to England. He would return in the winter. 'My father and mother are yet living, whom I am very anxious to see, and have informed them of my coming over the ensuing summer.'[4] A few days later he asked Franklin for letters of introduction. Franklin obliged, writing to a range of French scientists and politicians and to Jefferson, now America's minister to France. Paine's friend Henry Laurens recommended him to Edmund Burke, a Whig politician who had been an early critic of British policy in the American colonies.

Paine left for France on 26 April 1787. A month later the Philadelphia Convention held its first session to formulate a Constitution, presided over by Washington. Despite the part he had played in the independence struggle, Paine was neither offered nor sought a place as a delegate. Others, and Paine himself, realised his talent was for agitation, for forcing the break, not the dull grind of political construction. When proceedings ended on 17 September, the Convention had drafted the United States Constitution.

Soon after Paine made an observation on the destiny of nations. 'A thousand years hence ... perhaps in less, America may be what England now is! The innocence of her character that won the hearts of all nations in her favor may sound like romance, and inimitable virtue as if it had never been.'5

Paine devoted his attention over the next two years to seeking financial backing for his bridge, drawing almost every contact he made in France and England into the enterprise. But, almost despite himself, he was pulled into British and French politics. Now 50, he landed at Le Havre on 26 May 1787, going on to Paris. Jefferson was in Italy, but Franklin's letters opened doors. Paine told Franklin in June that he had received numerous visits and invitations. Lafayette, whom Paine had first met in Philadelphia in 1780, welcomed him into his circle of aristocrats and intellectuals, among them the Marquis de Condorcet, a mathematician, a radical thinker and a member of the Academy.

Paine, as on his landing in America in 1774, had arrived in the midst of historical drama. The budget had revealed France's dire economic state, with half the government's revenue going to service the national debt. On 21 February Louis XVI's finance minister proposed more extensive taxation to the Assembly of Notables, which was made up of aristocrats and senior churchmen. Lafayette, an Assembly member, objected and declared that royal extravagance was the source of France's problems. On 25 May the King dismissed the Assembly, turning to the regional parliaments for support. However, the Paris parliament insisted that only the Estates-General, which had not met since 1614, could levy new taxes.

Jefferson returned to Paris in late June. He and Paine began a friendly relationship as it emerged in long conversations that they shared an interest in the natural sciences and were politically sympathetic. Through Jefferson Paine met Jean-Baptiste Le Roy, a scientist. Le Roy, who spoke English and spent much time with Paine, who had no French, found Paine stimulating, writing to a friend, 'His intelligence upholds its reputation perfectly', and remarking on 'the honest and profound spirit which he brings to bear upon every subject.'6 Paine presented his model to the Academy on 21 July and was happy to find that Le Roy was chairman of the committee deputed to consider the design. On 29 August the committee reported that Paine's design was 'ingeniously imagined' and the model 'simple, solid and proper'.

Paine left at once for London with his model, hoping for a similar endorsement from the Royal Society, his imagination soaring with visions of bridges to his design constructed across the Seine, the Thames, even the English Channel. Jefferson gave Paine letters to carry, one to John Adams, now the American Minister in London, and one to a painter, John Trumbull, suggesting he arranged a portrait of Paine. The British government appeared forgiving of Paine's role in losing her American empire, and showed no interest in him.

Despite his preoccupation with the bridge, Paine's fears of a conflict between Britain and France over civil war in the Netherlands prompted him to write *Prospects on the Rubicon*, in the summer of 1787. The 67-page pamphlet had none of the impact of Paine's previous publications and sold few copies. Paine attacked those who thrived on rumours of war. 'There are thousands who live by it; it is their harvest, and the clamor which those people keep up in newspapers and conversations passes unsuspiciously for the voice of the people, and it is not till after the mischief is done that the deception is discovered.' He warned of war's unpredictability. 'It has but one thing certain, and that is to increase taxes … I defend the cause of the poor, of the manufacturer, of the tradesman, of the farmer, and of all those on whom the real burden of taxes fall – but above all, I defend the cause of humanity.'[7]

In England Paine tried, with no success, to interest the Marquis of Lansdowne, the Duke of Portland and the MP Edmund Burke in the bridge. But he also talked politics with Burke, beginning what promised to be a firm friendship. Born in Dublin, Burke had entered Parliament in 1765 and was active in the campaign to limit the powers of the monarchy. He had opposed the government treatment of the American colonists, and though no supporter of independence, showed some sympathy. Burke went with Paine to the Midlands to seek out sources of iron for his bridge but it was what appeared to be, on the surface at least, a shared desire for reform that bound them together. Burke told the radical John Wilkes, now Mayor of London, that he and Paine seemed to be in constant contact with one another.

Paine travelled to Thetford to find his mother, now in her nineties, alone. His father had died at the age of 78 and had been buried in November the previous year. His mother showed some pride in Paine's achievements in America, telling him that when she had read Congress had called a fast for 4 July, the anniversary of the Declaration of Independence, she had kept it strictly. Paine arranged for part of his income to be devoted to paying her a pension of nine shillings a week. This was the last time he saw his mother, who died in May 1790.

On his return to London Paine attended parties at the home of the painter Trumbull, who had served in the Continental Army and had gathered a circle of expatriate Americans around him. A fellow guest, Royall Tyler, described Paine as 'a spare man, rather under size; subject to the extreme of low, and highly exhilarating spirits; often sat reserved in company; seldom mingled in common chit chat: But when a man of sense and elocution was present, and the company numerous, he delighted in advancing the most unaccountable, and often the most whimsical paradoxes; which he defended in his own plausible manner'.[8] Then he would fall silent. Paine was aware of his loneliness, though in Paris he resisted the vigorous attempts of a baroness, Cornélie de Vasse, a friend of Lafayette's, to draw him into a more intimate relationship. He was to write to Kitty, the daughter of his New York friend Commodore Nicholson, on the occasion of her marriage, 'Though I appear a sort of wanderer, the married state has not a sincerer friend than I am. It is the harbour of human life ... It is home; and that one word conveys more than any other word can express.'[9]

Paine continued his inconclusive and frustrating journeying between London and Paris promoting the bridge. But America was not entirely off his mind. On 21 June 1788 the new Constitution was formally adopted in the United States. Paine told Jefferson and Lafayette that were he in America he would certainly support it, though he was concerned at the power placed in the President's hands.

When Adams returned to the United States Paine, with Jefferson's encouragement, became the country's semi-official representative in London, gathering political intelligence for Jefferson to pass to his government. Paine extended his acquaintance among Whig politicians, discussing affairs with Charles James Fox, the Marquis of Lansdowne and the Duke of Portland, opposition leaders sharing some of his liberal views. Paine gave Jefferson the benefit of his opinions on developments in London, confident in both his right and his ability to do so. In November 1788 George III became temporarily insane. William Pitt, the prime minister, proposed appointing George's son as Regent. Paine disagreed, writing to Jefferson that now was the time for Britain to seize the opportunity the King's illness presented. Britain should follow America and call a national convention to establish a new constitution, an unlikely event, as Paine knew.

In April 1789 Paine negotiated a contract with an ironworks in Yorkshire to construct a full-scale bridge with a single arch spanning 110 feet. He hoped to persuade a private investor to erect it over the Thames. But Paine was running short of ready cash and on 13 July wrote to Jefferson asking advice on transferring funds from America. The iron founders eventually built a bridge to Paine's design, though he received no payment. But by then he had a fresh inspiration, a rekindling of what he would call 'the ardour of seventy-six'.[10] On 14 July the Parisians stormed the Bastille.

REFLECTIONS ON THE REVOLUTION

15

The consequences of Louis XVI's agreement to summon the Estates-General were dramatic and unforeseen. Within three months, France had undergone a revolution at least as far-reaching in its effects as America's. The Estates-General (with the First Estate representing the clergy, the Second Estate the aristocracy, and the Third Estate the commoners) were unable to reach agreement on the King's reforms. On 11 May 1789 the Third Estate broke away and, supported by a sprinkling of liberal aristocrats and members of the clergy, declared themselves the National Assembly, representatives of the 'people' as a whole. The next step was to draft a new constitution.

Urged on by conservative advisors, Louis attempted to maintain his hold on power by recasting the ministry. The people of Paris interpreted this as a threat to their revolution and to the National Assembly. On 14 July demonstrators seized and demolished the fortified Bastille prison with support from soldiers, some of whom had served in America. Paine's friend Lafayette took command of the National Guard, a 'people's army', symbolising the part the liberal aristocracy was playing in this phase of the revolution. With the fall of the Bastille, the National Assembly became France's effective government as revolutionary fervour erupted through the provinces. On 4 August the National Assembly abolished feudalism, shattering with one blow the traditional powers of the nobility and the church, going on to proclaim a 'Declaration of the Rights of Man and of the Citizen'. In November the National Assembly confiscated the church's lands.

As a connoisseur of revolution following his exploits in America, Paine could not contain his enthusiasm. In September, writing to Jefferson, he grasped at the opportunity events in France might present to the people of Britain. 'There is yet in this country very considerable remains of the feudal system which people did not see before the Revolution in France placed it before their eyes ... [T]hey appear to me to be turning their eyes towards the aristocrats of their own nation.'[1] He wrote to Washington in October, 'To have a share in two revolutions is living to some purpose.'[2]

Paine travelled to a transformed France in November. Under the influence of Lafayette and those around him, the country was turning to a constitutional monarchy. In Paris, Paine's companions were Lafayette, Condorcet and other figures prominent in leading the changes. But his closest friend over the winter was Thomas Christie, the young nephew of the radical English scientist Joseph Priestley. Christie would go on in 1792 to become a founder member of the London Corresponding Society, a revolutionary organisation whose members took Paine as their inspiration.

Jefferson had returned to the United States in September. Lafayette and his co-leaders in Paris acknowledged Paine as the American Revolution personified, presenting him with the key to the Bastille to pass to Washington, the President of the country they admired. But Gouverneur Morris, in France on private business, retained his low opinion of Paine (though Paine seemed completely oblivious) and was not slow to voice it. On 26 January 1790 Lafayette told Morris he wished to meet him and Paine. Morris noted in his diary, 'I tell him that Paine can do him no good, for that, although he has an excellent pen, he has but an indifferent head to think.'[3]

Paine wrote to Burke in London on 17 January, expressing his delight at the almost bloodless overthrow of feudalism in France and the promise of a popular constitution. His friend, however, was horrified at the dangers revolution presented to both France and Britain. Paine described schoolboys marching in the streets carrying muskets, crying that they were emulating the men of America. 'The Revolution in France is certainly a forerunner to other revolutions in Europe.'[4] Burke replied angrily that the actions of the French would be destructive of all constitutional government. After reading his response, Paine was not surprised to hear that Burke was proposing to write a pamphlet critical of the revolution.

Paine went to London on 17 March 1790 to oversee further arrangements with his iron bridge. In May he sent Washington the key that Lafayette had given him. Paine made it clear to the President that, in the case of Louis (whom he would call 'a man of a good heart'), he had lost his aversion to monarchs, and suggested that Washington might wish to 'congratulate the King and Queen of France (for they have been our friends), and the National Assembly, on the happy example they are giving to Europe'.[5] He was disturbed by news of the deployment of Lafayette's National Guard to put down rioting in Paris, but saw this as part of the inevitable turmoil of political change.

Paine mixed with American, and also French, *émigrés* in London but as the impact of events in France heightened in Britain his contacts with sympathisers of the revolution grew. The radical Charles James Fox, for example, did not for the moment share Burke's horror at its implications. Paine discussed the revolution and the possible repercussions for Britain with the feminist Mary Wollstonecraft and her future husband, the anarchist William Godwin. Paine had been made an honorary member of the Society for Constitutional Information in 1787, though he had not known it at the time. In the new atmosphere the Society, whose meetings Paine now attended, pressed their demands for annual parliaments, equal representation and a restoration of the liberties they believed had existed before the Norman Conquest. Paine also spent much time with Gouverneur Morris, who, to Paine's disappointment had now replaced him as the United States' unofficial representative in London. Paine appeared as careless with other people's money as with his own, Morris noting in his diary on 14 August 1790, 'Paine calls on me to borrow money, being as he says too much fatigued to go into the city. I lend him three guineas which I fancy will not be speedily repaid.'[6]

Paine returned briefly to Paris in October 1790, returning when he heard that Burke's long-awaited blast against the revolution was about to appear. *Reflections on the Revolution in France* was published on 1 November. Paine had already decided he would respond, promising his friends in France that his defence of their revolution would not be slow in coming. He began writing in his lodgings at the Angel Inn, Islington, a few days after Burke's work had been published.

Burke had been alarmed by the seizure of the Bastille, reminiscent to him of the Gordon Riots that had devastated much of London in 1780. He had been angered by a sermon delivered by the Dissenting preacher Dr

Richard Price on the anniversary of the Glorious Revolution of 1688. Price had seen in France and America the birth of a new world, one in which he sensed 'the ardour for liberty catching and spreading ... the dominion of kings changed for the dominion of laws, and the dominion of priests giving way to the dominion of reason and conscience'.[7] Paine could not but admire a man who echoed his own thoughts so closely and the two had dined together in London. But for Burke, the call for Britain to emulate France was to open the way for the abandonment of all tradition and custom and an end to the deference he saw as the bond holding society together. Lyrical and at times sentimental – as in his regret for the indignities he feared had been inflicted on the French Queen, Marie Antoinette – Burke's *Reflections* was a conservative manifesto, a warning of the dangers of power falling into the hands of the 'swinish multitude'. First anarchy, then dictatorship. The traditions handed down from the past were wiser than cries for the rights of man. Burke succeeded in polarising attitudes towards the French Revolution and sharpening the fault line in British politics between conservatism and reform. A former radical Whig (*Reflections* lost him many Whig allies), his words were now welcomed by conservatives and the King, who recommended Burke's pamphlet to 'every gentleman'. Burke had written provocatively, 'Kings will be tyrants from policy when subjects are rebels from principle.'

The intellectual counter-attack was rapid. At the end of November Mary Wollstonecraft opened fire with *A Vindication of the Rights of Man* (followed in 1792 by *A Vindication of the Rights of Women*) and further sallies came from Joseph Priestley and Thomas Christie. But it was Paine's promised response that the radical world awaited. He had boasted that he could counter Burke in four days, and alleged Burke had written in the service of the Crown, a charge that seemed justified when it emerged that the King had awarded Burke a pension. Paine's 40,000 word reply – *Rights of Man: Being An Answer to Mr Burke's Attack on the French Revolution* – took a little over three months to compose.

RIGHTS OF MAN, PART ONE

16

Paine completed the first part of *Rights of Man* on 29 January 1791, his 54th birthday. He passed the manuscript to a printer, Joseph Johnson, who promised publication on 22 February, the birthday of Washington, to whom Paine had dedicated the work. But the government already appeared alarmed at the dangers of Paine's pen and its agents pressured Johnson to delay. Paine entered into a new agreement with another printer, the radical J S Jordan. Paine then went to Paris, leaving final arrangements in the hands of Godwin and two radical friends. He returned to London a few days before *Rights of Man* appeared on 13 March at a price of three shillings. Paine was to earn nothing, the proceeds going to the Society for Constitutional Information.

As with *Common Sense* 15 years previously, Paine had set himself two tasks. The first was to answer Burke's criticisms of the French Revolution. The second was to draw broader conclusions about its significance for Britain and the world. Paine wrote with a confidence that he understood the future, while Burke could see only an eternal past. He dismissed Burke with a sarcasm that derived from his disappointment at the reasons for the end to their friendship. 'I know a place in America called Point-no-Point; because as you proceed along the shore, gay and flowery as Mr Burke's language, it continually recedes and presents itself at a distance before you; but when you have got as far as you can go, there is no point at all. Just thus it is with Mr Burke's three hundred and fifty six pages.'[1]

He accused Burke of omission and distortion, of striving for effect. Burke might claim to write in defence of a principle but he was, Paine alleged, writing for personal advantage, the pension from the King. Paine set out his own history of the revolution, based on observation and what he had learned from the leading participants. 'Notwithstanding Mr Burke's horrid paintings, when the French Revolution is compared with the revolutions of other countries, the astonishment will be, that it is marked with so few sacrifices; but this astonishment will cease when we reflect that principles, and not persons, were the mediated objects of destruction.' By exposing what he saw as Burke's ignorance and misapprehensions about events in France, Paine hoped to draw his readers to the conclusion that Burke's conservative politics were at fault. 'Whom has the National Assembly brought to the scaffold? None.'[2] France would move in the direction Burke feared, as Paine found to his own cost. But for the moment the revolution opened a new era, an age of reason, one in which privilege and tradition would be overthrown and natural and civil rights would gain universal recognition. The repressed would free themselves. Burke might bemoan Marie Antoinette's humiliation at the hands of the revolutionaries but, Paine replied, 'He pities the plumage, but forgets the dying bird … His hero or heroine must be a tragedy-victim expiring in show, and not the real prisoner of misery, sliding into death in the silence of a dungeon.'[3]

Burke had denied any human right beyond that of being governed in accordance with tradition and precedent. Paine defended liberty and equality against the burden of history. 'The vanity and presumption of governing beyond the grave, is the most ridiculous and insolent of all tyrannies.' The people in every age could choose whatever form of government they wished. 'If any generation of men ever possessed the right of dictating the mode by which the world should be governed for ever, it was the first generation that existed; and if that generation did it not, no succeeding generation can shew any authority for doing it, nor can set any up'. All men were equal since 'every child born into the world must be considered as deriving its existence from God. The world is as new to him as it was to the first man that ever existed, and his natural right in it is of the same kind.'[4]

Burke had spoken of the constitution governing Britain's affairs. Paine asked to see that constitution. Could Burke produce it? 'If he cannot, we may fairly conclude that though it has been so much talked about, no such thing as a constitution exists, or ever did exist, and consequently that the people have yet a constitution to form.'[5] He contrasted the new system of government in revolutionary France, the assemblies elected by universal suffrage, the equal constituencies, the religious freedom, with Britain's rotten boroughs, seven-year parliaments and the persecution of Dissenters.

Paine pointed, as he had in *Common Sense*, to the fallacy of hereditary rule, of monarchy and nobility (the 'No-ability'), which, he said, was 'as inconsistent as that of hereditary judges, or hereditary juries; and as absurd as an hereditary mathematician, or an hereditary wise man; and as ridiculous as an hereditary poet-laureate'. The American and the French revolutions had cast a beam of light across the world by which all men could see. 'Ignorance is of a peculiar nature: once dispelled, it is impossible to re-establish it. It is not originally a thing of itself, but is only the absence of knowledge and though a man may be kept ignorant, he cannot be made ignorant ... it has never yet been discovered, how to make a man unknow his knowledge, or unthink his thoughts.' Paine described what made the French and American revolutions novel. In the past a revolution had meant simply a change of rulers. But the revolutions of this age were 'a renovation of the natural order of things, a system of principles as universal as truth, and the existence of man, and combining moral with political happiness and national prosperity'.[6]

With *Common Sense*, Paine had invented a fresh style of journalism, putting the complexity of political argument within the reach of any reader. *Rights of Man* introduced that style to Britain, to Burke's 'swinish multitude'. Paine's argument moved from Burke, to France, to Britain, to universal principles. Though he wrote vividly, he was saying little that was unfamiliar to those who had read Locke and understood republican thought. But, beyond America and, for the moment, France, no country strove to work according to those precepts. In *Common Sense*, and in an American context, Paine had joined republicanism and anti-monarchism. Now he appeared to accept in Louis of France that a monarch and republican principles were compatible. Where did that place the King in Britain? With optimism reminiscent of 1776, Paine wrote, 'It is an age of Revolutions, in which every thing may be looked for.'[7]

The first edition sold out in a matter of hours and by the end of May *Rights of Man* had gone into a sixth edition, selling faster than any previous publication in Britain. The circulation went over 50,000 in three months. Paine was flooded with requests for permission to reprint cheaper editions, to which he agreed, foregoing royalties to ensure a low cover price. In April

Paine decided to produce his own cheap edition, the price covering only the cost of paper and printing, though he feared this might lead to his arrest. The *Gazetteer and London Daily Advertiser* reported that the government's law officers were considering prosecuting him for sedition, but had yet to decide. Even the King was said to have leafed through a copy of Paine's work in a bookshop near Windsor Castle, stopping reading when he reached a passage that compared the role of the monarch unfavourably with that of a local constable.[8]

Rather than the bludgeon of prosecution, the government devised a subtler means of undermining Paine's reputation, hiring George Chalmers, a lawyer and writer, to concoct a biography. Chalmers, who had lived in Maryland and had opposed the struggle for American independence, was now working at the Board of Trade. He drew together what information he could gather, true or not, presenting it under the pen name Francis Oldys in *Life of Thomas Pain; the Author of The Rights of Men, with a Defence of His Writings*. The title was carefully phrased and shielded the book's true purpose, which was to counter Paine's arguments by revealing the failures and disappointments of his life. Paine, hurt by the accusations Chalmers made – for example, that he had ill-treated his first wife – remained silent, a controversial figure whose politics could only be answered with the bitterest of personal abuse.

The impact of *Rights of Man* was international as translations were published in France, Holland and the German kingdoms and principalities. An American edition appeared in May 1791 with an unauthorised preface by Jefferson, now Secretary of State in Washington's administration. Publication of the preface threatened Jefferson's already difficult relations with Vice-President Adams, a prominent figure among the pro-British and anti-French Federalists. Despite his embarrassment, Jefferson congratulated Paine in July that *Rights of Man* had 'checked the advance' of those in America who were 'preaching up and panting after an English constitution of king, lords and commons, and whose heads are itching for crowns, coronets, and mitres'.[9] Jefferson, James Madison and the Attorney General, Edmund Randolph, lobbied Washington – with no success – to appoint Paine to the vacant office of Postmaster-General. Paine appears to have known nothing of this. Washington ignored a gift of a dozen copies of *Rights of Man* that Paine had sent, replying grudgingly almost a year later.

Paine had returned to London on 7 March 1791 but almost immediately went back to France. He stayed first in Paris with an American acquaintance who, as he told Gouverneur Morris, found him a 'little mad'. Morris agreed. Paine's madness was perhaps exhilaration at his regained notoriety.

A Frenchman who travelled briefly with Paine, Étienne Dumont, described him as 'drunk with vanity. If you believed him, it was he who had done everything in America'. Dumont said Paine had declared that if it were in his power he would destroy every book in existence and leave only *Rights of Man* for the world to read. 'He knew all his own writings by heart,' Dumont reported, 'but he knew nothing else.'[10] Dumont was no admirer of Paine, but others had made similar comments about the effect of fame on a man who, for all his talents, had about him the air of a permanent outsider.

Paine moved on to Versailles, where he stayed at Lafayette's home, making early drafts of a second part to *Rights of Man*, which he proposed calling *Kingship*. On 22 June 1791 Lafayette burst into Paine's room shouting, 'The birds have flown'. The King and Queen, disguised as a valet and a governess, had fled Paris towards the border where they hoped to seek shelter with the Austrian army. Paine, angry at what he saw as the King's treachery to the revolution, told Lafayette that he hoped there would be no attempt to bring them back. They were recaptured at Varennes and Paine watched their return to Paris under arrest on 25 June. Observing the crowds that had gathered to jeer, Paine told his friend Christie, 'You see the absurdity of monarchical governments. Here will be a whole nation disturbed by the folly of one man.'[11]

Paine himself almost became a victim of popular feeling against the monarchy on the day of the King's return. Walking through the streets without the obligatory revolutionary tricolour cockade in his hat, he was accused of being an aristocrat and narrowly escaped being hanged from a lamp-post. Paine had seen the French Revolution as the American Revolution acted out in Europe, with all the simplicity and purity of 1776. Now he would experience the dark and confused passions that could arise from a long-repressed anger. Nevertheless, as Part Two of the *Rights of Man* would show, Paine clung to his hopes of democratic revolution.

ENGLAND IS NOT YET FREE

17

Following the royal flight and recapture, opinion in France, until now willing to accept Louis as a constitutional monarch, began to move against the principle of kingship. Condorcet (whom Paine had first met as an aristocratic member of the Academy of Sciences in 1787) turned to republicanism immediately. With Nicholas de Bonneville (a journalist and printer), Jacques-Pierre Brissot de Warville (a journalist and Assembly member) and Achille du Châtelet (a liberal former aristocrat), Condorcet established the Republican Society and a short-lived newspaper, *Le Républicain*, the first in France to advocate an end to monarchy. Paine, who was acquainted with Brissot as well as Condorcet, asked to join them, saying that despite his lack of French he would write for the newspaper under the pen-name 'Common Sense'. Paine contributed to, if he did not write entirely, the Society's manifesto, which he and du Châtelet posted on buildings throughout Paris, including the National Assembly, where a deputy angrily pulled it from the wall. The manifesto declared that the King, whom it described as 'Louis Capet', had effectively abdicated by fleeing the throne and thereby breaking his oath of office. Louis was condemned as a 'miserable creature who is conscious of his own dishonour', but the Society argued against seeking revenge against the Royal Family.

The manifesto generated debate in the National Assembly but, as yet, the majority of its members were unwilling to go as far as abolishing the monarchy. One supposed supporter of Louis argued in *Le Moniteur* that kings were necessary because they defended society from tyranny and society was therefore freer under a monarchy. Paine responded in the paper's pages that, contrary to his earlier opinion, he now saw that a nation with a king had no claim to the title republic. He charged monarchy as a system with responsibility for all of history's wars and massacres, but insisted he had no personal enmity to kings. 'Quite the contrary. No man wishes more heartily than myself to see them all in a happy and honourable state of private individuals; but I am the avowed, open, and intrepid enemy of what is called monarchy …'[1]

Paine and his fellow republican Condorcet were increasingly of one mind and jointly drafted an essay, *Answer to Four Questions on the Legislative and Executive Powers*, published in 1792. They called for a national convention to resolve the growing constitutional crisis. This was to be followed by a wider conference of 'the representatives of the various nations of Europe, which would adopt measures for the general welfare. The felicity which liberty insures us is transformed into virtue when we communicate its enjoyment to others.'[2] Part Two of *Rights of Man* would show how far working on this essay with Condorcet had carried Paine's thinking about the roots of poverty and government's role in society. As far as Gouverneur Morris was concerned Paine was letting his enthusiasm carry him away. After a dinner of Americans in Paris celebrating Independence Day on 4 July 1791, Morris commented in his diary that Paine was 'inflated to the eyes and big with a litter of revolutions'.[3]

Paine was now preparing to return to London, where his arrival was expected with excitement and foreboding following the success of the first part of *Rights of Man*. Enterprising printers had brought out copies of *The American Crisis 12* and *13*, both of which found a ready market. A newspaper, *The Oracle*, reported on 8 July that Paine was busily engaged in writing his new pamphlet, *Kingship*. This would appear in November in simultaneous English, French, German, Italian and Spanish editions. 'Such is the rage for disseminating democratic principles!'[4] This was astute publicity for the forthcoming work, whetting the public taste for further controversy, and presumably emanated from Paine. The British Minister in France, the Earl of Gower, reported in a dispatch to the Home Secretary, Lord Grenville, that Paine intended making mischief in England and Ireland. Another peer, the Earl of Mornington, demanded of Lord Grenville that Paine be indicted for his flagrant libel in *Rights of Man* of the King, the House of Lords and the House of Commons.

Paine arrived in London on 13 July 1791 and was immediately confined to bed with exhaustion. In August he moved into the Marylebone Street home of his friend 'Clio' Rickman, an admirer of Paine's since they had met in Lewes 20 years before, and now a prosperous bookseller. Paine spent much of the late summer and autumn at Rickman's house writing Part Two of *Rights of Man*. Rickman noted of Paine that though broad-shouldered and athletic, he now stooped a little. 'In his dress and person he was generally very cleanly, and wore his hair cued, with side curls, and powdered, so that he looked like a gentleman of the old French school. His manners were easy and gracious; his knowledge was universal and boundless; in private company and among his friends his conversation had every fascination that anecdote, novelty and truth could give it. In mixt company and among strangers he said little, and was no public speaker.'[5]

This would be Paine's last year in England and possibly the happiest he had known in the country. He was financially secure, comfortable with Rickman's family, living a settled life, eating and sleeping regularly, playing chess, dominoes and draughts in the evenings. Paine strolled and idled in coffee houses, visiting and talking to a wide range of friends and acquaintances, including the American and French ambassadors, Wollstonecraft, Godwin, Priestley and John Horne Took, a radical writer and chairman of the Society for Constitutional Information. Paine sat for a portrait by George Romney, now lost. An engraving from the portrait by William Sharp survives, showing Paine at 55, with greying hair, alert eyes and a prominent nose. His jaw is determined, the set of his mouth sardonic.

On 20 August Paine addressed a meeting organised by the Friends of Universal Peace and Liberty in a tavern off Piccadilly. 'We congratulate the French nation for having laid the axe to the root of tyranny, and for erecting government on the sacred hereditary rights of man; rights which appertain to all, and not to any one more than another … Beneath the feudal system all Europe has long groaned, and from it England is not yet free.'[6] But what Paine and London were waiting for was Burke's response to *Rights of Man*. Burke's *Appeal from the New to the Old Whigs* was published shortly after Paine's speech. He treated Paine with contempt, not once referring to him by name. He said he would not attempt 'in the smallest degree' to counter the arguments set out in *Rights of Man*. 'This will probably be done (if such writings shall be thought to deserve any other than the refutation of criminal justice) by others.'[7]

The clash between Paine and Burke symbolised the complex political divisions developing in Britain in the wake of the French Revolution. Membership of organisations for conservatism, reform and radical change multiplied as agitational energy shifted from the élites to the masses, and in 1790 a Manchester clergyman had established a 'Church and King' dining club. In July 1791 a mob under that banner had attacked Priestley's home in Birmingham, destroying his laboratory and going on to sack three Dissenting meeting houses in a confused orgy of patriotism and loyalty to Anglicanism. In January 1792 a Scottish shoemaker, Thomas Hardy, formed the London Corresponding Society to link the work of similar radical clubs that had been formed throughout the country. In London, the artist William Blake injected a visionary element into the ferment of ideas and dreams.

Paine was made an icon, positive or negative depending on political opinion. In 1792 the government paid John Bowles, as it had paid Chalmers, to publish *A Protest against Tom Paine's Rights of Man*. In November the government funded the formation of an Association for Preserving Liberty and Property against Republicans and Levellers. The Association would go on to organise demonstrations at which Paine was burnt in effigy to the singing of the National Anthem and chanting of 'Up with the cause of old England; And down with the tricks of Tom Paine'.

Paine's writing was going slowly and his earlier hopes of finishing by November faded. He had never found the process of writing easy. But Paine was determined that his latest work would shock his opponents and rally his supporters. On 2 November 1791 he wrote to the American chargé d'affaires in Paris, 'I have but one way to go to be secure in my next work which is, to go further than in my first. I see that great rogues escape by the excess of their crimes, and, perhaps, it may be the same in honest cases.'[8]

As the book neared completion both Johnson and Jordan, who had been involved with the first part of *Rights of Man*, were reluctant to play any part in publication. Thomas Chapman, a radical admirer of Paine's, agreed to publish the work, offering 5,000 and then 1,000 guineas for the copyright. Paine refused, preferring to retain all rights. But when Chapman read what Paine had so far written, he too had second thoughts, though he hesitated in telling Paine. On 16 January 1792 Paine burst into the print shop drunk, which Chapman thought unusual. There was an argument involving religion, in the course of which Paine insulted Mrs Chapman, giving Chapman the opportunity to pull out of the venture. Paine, who tried to apologise next day, concluded Chapman had been under pressure from government agents. Paine now returned to Jordan, promising in writing that he would take personal responsibility for any trouble the book's publication might cause. On that basis, *Rights of Man Part the Second, combining Principle and Practice* went on sale on 16 February at a price of three shillings, with a first printing of 5,000. The work was dedicated to Paine's friend Lafayette in gratitude for his service to 'my beloved America'. Within a fortnight the book had gone through four printings. An elated Paine spoke to Gouverneur Morris on the day of publication. Morris recorded in his diary, 'He seems cocksure of bringing about a revolution in Great Britain and I think it quite as likely that he will be promoted to the pillory.'[9]

RIGHTS OF MAN, PART TWO

18

Paine's purpose in the second part of *Rights of Man* was, as he described in the title, to combine principle and practice. He noted Burke's failure to address his arguments, setting out the familiar description of the role of civil society and government, with a practised wit and abuse of the Crown, '[T]he master fraud that shelters all others'. Monarchy, he said, '[A]lways appears to me a silly, contemptible thing. I compare it to something kept behind a curtain, about which there is a great deal of bustle and fuss, and a wonderful air of seeming solemnity; but when, by any accident, the curtain happens to be open, and the company see what it is, they burst into laughter.'[1] Paine expressed genuine surprise at accusations that he was a leveller. The only levelling he had seen was in monarchy, a mental levelling. 'Kings succeed each other, not as rationals but as animals.' He mocked the British royal family's German origins. 'A foreigner cannot be a member of parliament, but he may be what is called a king.'[2] He was confident that within seven years no crowned head or aristocrat would remain in Europe.

Government, Paine said, was no more than a national association to secure the good of all, individually and collectively. 'Every man wishes to pursue his occupation, and to enjoy the fruits of his labours, and the produce of his property in peace and safety, and with the least possible expense. When these things are accomplished, all the objects for which government ought to be established are answered.' With a democratic representative government, every matter was open and the concern of all. Citizens in such a republic would not 'adopt the slavish system of following what in other governments are called LEADERS'.[3]

Then, in the fifth chapter, Paine set out the practice he had promised. He described a scheme of universal social security financed through taxation, not perhaps a welfare state but one in which government took some action in the interest of all citizens. The chapter rings with Paine's own experience, his origins in England's lower class. Paine had triumphed in America, but every fear and hurt he had endured in England remained vivid. Poverty, he argued, was not a phenomenon of nature but a creation of man. 'When it shall be said in any country in the world, my poor are happy; neither ignorance nor distress is to be found among them; my jails are empty of prisoners, my streets of beggars; the aged are not in want, the taxes are not oppressive; the rational world is my friend, because I am the friend of its happiness: when these things can be said, then may that country boast its constitution and its government.'[4]

Paine identified the poor as large families, and the elderly unable to work. They were entitled to support not as charity but as a right. They were paying taxes on all they consumed, but scarcely a 40th part went to what he called civil government, the remainder going on war, preparations for war and support of a parasitic aristocracy. A labouring man with a wife and children paid, Paine estimated, £8 or £9 in tax a year and was, as a consequence, unable to provide for his family if he were taken sick. Paine proposed a grant of £4 a year for every child under 14, to be spent on education in reading, writing and arithmetic. 'By adopting this method, not only the poverty of the parents will be relieved, but ignorance will be banished, and the number of poor will hereafter become less, because their abilities, by the aid of education, will be greater.'[5] Every woman was to receive a grant of £1 on giving birth, and the same sum awarded to each newly-married couple. The retirement age was to be 60, with a pension of £10 a year. Those between 50 and 60, whose powers to work were weakening, would have a pension of £6 per annum. 'It is painful to see old age working itself to death, in what are called civilized countries, for daily bread.'[6] There were to be allowances for demobilised sailors and soldiers, a wage increase for Excise officers, and hostels for workers travelling the country in search of employment. Taxation would shift from the poor rate and levies on consumption to a progressive tax on land and what it yielded to its owners. Paine showed the cost of each of his proposals and set out in every case how money would be found to pay. He suggested there could even be a reduction of tax overall.

There would be benefits to the whole of society, Paine argued. The punitive Poor Laws and the workhouses they created, which he called 'instruments of civil torture', would be abolished. Humane hearts would no longer be shocked by the sight of ragged, hungry children and elderly men and women who were forced to beg. The birth of a child would be seen as a cause for joy rather than despair. Petty crime, 'the offspring of distress and poverty', would lessen. Society would know it had an interest in government and 'the cause and apprehension of riots and tumults will cease'.[7] Paine's proposals were breathtaking for their time. Indeed, nothing even resembling them was attempted in Britain for another 150 years.

But Paine was no socialist and was not advocating a transformation of the economic system. He respected the rights of property, accepted the market mechanism and believed that trade encouraged peace. Like Condorcet, Paine opposed monopoly and ownership of large estates; neither appeared to see the industrial capitalism being born behind their backs, despite Paine's visits to the Midlands' iron foundries. What Paine envisaged was equality, guaranteed by a democratic state through redistributive taxation, social security and education. Government would be minimal, ensuring provision only where civil society could not. At one point he approached anarchism, now apparently more optimistic about society's possibilities than he had been in *Common Sense*. Citing his experience of the early stages of the American Revolution, Paine wrote, 'The instant formal government is abolished, society begins to act. A general association takes place, and common interest produces common security ... The more perfect civilization is, the less occasion has it for government, because the more does it regulate its own affairs, and govern itself.'[8]

By the end of 1792 over 200,000 copies of the second part of *Rights of Man* were circulating in Britain alone, helped by the almost immediate issue of a cheap edition. (Burke's *Reflections* sold only 30,000 copies in two years.) Paine's ability to connect political reform with a specific programme for social change, and the plain language in which he phrased this, won him new admirers and sharpened the division between those who thought in terms of minor reforms and those favouring radical steps. Paine's allies reworded the National Anthem, though they could not but acknowledge that the revolution faced determined enemies in the streets as well as the palaces.

'God save great Thomas Paine
His Rights of Man explain
To every soul.
He makes the blind to see
What dupes and slaves they be,
And points out liberty,
From pole to pole.

Thousands cry 'Church and King'
That well deserve to swing,
All must allow.
Birmingham blush for shame,
Manchester do the same,
Infamous is your name,
Patriots vow.'

In April 1792 Paine moved temporarily to Bromley, a village south of
London, to stay with the engraver William Sharp. On a visit to London
to attend a meeting of the Society for Constitutional Information, he was
arrested at a tavern door over a complicated debt connected with his iron
bridge. Paine was thrown into the debtors' prison at King's Head but bailed
next day by Johnson, the printer who had withdrawn from involvement
in publishing the first part of *Rights of Man*. Stories about the 'republican
debtor' found their way into the press, suggesting a campaign of harassment
had begun. Such was the government's concern at the possible effect of
Rights of Man, the Secretary for War dispatched a senior officer to garrisons
across England to gauge the loyalty of the men who might have to be
deployed against any rising.

On 14 May Paine's publisher, Jordan, was indicted for issuing a seditious
work. Paine hurried to London and urged Jordan to contest the charge,
promising to pay his legal expenses. Jordan refused, pleaded guilty and paid a
small fine. A week later a royal proclamation appeared, outlawing all 'wicked
and seditious writings', leading to raids on booksellers. On the same day,
Paine was summoned to appear in court in June on a charge of seditious
libel. He was described in the summons as 'Thomas Paine, late of London,
gentleman, being a wicked, malicious, seditious, and ill-disposed person,
and being greatly disaffected to our said Sovereign Lord the now King, and
to the happy constitution and government of this kingdom'.[9] The prime
minister, William Pitt, admitted to Charles James Fox in the Commons that
the proclamation had been aimed at Paine, who had written a book, Pitt

said, 'which struck at hereditary nobility, and which went to the destruction of monarchy and religion, and the total subversion of the established form of government.'[10]

Paine, shadowed by government agents, as he was aware, remained defiant. On 6 June he wrote a mocking open letter to the Home Secretary in which he called the King 'his Madjesty'. Paine's opponents stepped up demonstrations against him, hanging effigies in towns throughout England. He seemed delighted at the imminent confrontation, writing to the Manchester radical Walker, 'As we have now got the stone to roll, it must be kept going by cheap publications. This will embarrass the Court gentry more than anything else, because it is a ground they are not used to.'[11] Paine turned the screw more tightly with *Letter Addressed to the Addressers, On the Late Proclamation*, written at this time but appearing after he had left England. He ridiculed appealing to Parliament to reform itself, calling instead for a democratically-elected National Convention to establish a republican constitution for Britain. 'THE NATION WILL DECREE ITS OWN REFORMS; and the clamour about Party and Faction, or Ins and Outs, will become ridiculous.'[12]

Paine attended court on 8 June, to discover that his trial had been postponed until 18 December. The government were perhaps hoping that Paine would in the meantime leave the country, as his radical friend Priestley had done, emigrating to the United States. On 26 August the French National Assembly declared Paine an honorary citizen of France, along with others including Priestley, and the Americans Washington, Madison and Alexander Hamilton. Shortly after, Paine was elected by three departments as their delegate to the National Convention, charged with composing a new French Constitution. Though keen to face his accusers in court, Paine was flattered when the president of the National Assembly described him as a 'man of genius' and urged him to travel to France to 'give to her people a government the most proper to insure their liberty and happiness'.[13]

There is a story, unfortunately probably untrue, that Paine was warned by William Blake on 12 September to flee England. Blake is said to have laid his hand on Paine's shoulder as he was leaving a gathering at Johnson's house and whispered, 'You must not go home, or you are a dead man.'[14] Whatever the truth, Paine left London the following night with two companions, trailed by government agents who searched his room and luggage at Dover, confiscating a manuscript of *Letters to the Addressers*. Paine boarded the boat to France heckled by an angry crowd shouting "Down with the traitor' and 'Death to the corset maker'. This was the last he saw of England.

Paine's trial opened in his absence at Guildhall on 18 December before a jury guaranteed to follow the government's line. He had written in November to the Attorney General, Archibald Macdonald, regretting that his duties in France prevented his attendance, adding an insulting reference to the King, whom Paine called 'Mr Guelph', and declaring the British government to be 'a great, if not the greatest, perfection of fraud and corruption that ever took place since governments began'.[15] Macdonald gave the letter a prominent place in his opening address, to the dismay of Paine's counsel, Thomas Erskine, who had not known of its existence. Erskine did what he could, speaking for four hours in defence of the liberty of the press. But at the conclusion of his speech the jury foreman told the judge they needed to hear no more and declared Paine guilty, in effect exiling him on pain of imprisonment and possibly hanging should he return. Prosecutions soon began of booksellers handling Paine's works, including his friend Rickman, who fled to France. By 1797 all Paine's books had been banned in Britain and the number of prosecutions mounted.

Paine's nerves were shaken, a British government agent reporting from France that he had retired to the country for two days on the pretext of being unwell. Gouverneur Morris noted on Paine's return to Paris, 'Paine looks a little down at the news from England. He has been burnt in effigy.'[16]

AMONG SANGUINARY MEN

19

Paine's arrival in France could not have been a greater contrast to his flight from England. He landed in Calais, having accepted an invitation to serve as the department's deputy. Despite heavy rain, a battery of artillery fired a salute and the guard turned out for his inspection. Crowds cheered as Paine and his party made their way from the pier to an official welcome by the Constitutional Society at the town hall. To prolonged applause, Paine laid hand on heart and promised to devote his life to the French cause. A companion wrote to a friend in London, 'I believe he is rather fatigued with all the kissing.'[1] On 19 September 1792 Paine took a room at White's Hotel d'Angleterre in Paris, visited Gouverneur Morris, now American ambassador in France, and on 21 September registered as a deputy with the National Convention. He was, at 55, one of the older members and one of the few of working-class origin. These were not drawbacks, but being a foreigner with no practical political experience would prove disastrous.

On 20 April 1792 France had declared war on Austria and soon Prussia was drawn into the struggle. Sensing they were in a war for the revolution's survival, radical *sans-culottes* stormed the Tuileries in Paris on 10 August, driving out the King and Queen and demanding an end to the monarchy. (*Sans-culottes* were so called because they wore trousers rather than knee breeches to signify their enmity to aristocracy.) A more radical body dominated by Maximilien Robespierre and Louis-Antoine de St Just replaced the elected Paris commune, dispatching commissioners to every French department to press for revolutionary zeal. Under growing pressure, the National Assembly suspended Louis XVI as king and ordered elections to a National Convention to draw up a new constitution. France had experienced a second revolution. Suspected royalists were herded into jails where almost 2,000 prisoners were killed between 2 and 7 September. An ironic aspect would be that Paine was granted French citizenship and elected to the Convention as a symbol of the new militancy. Paine made no reference in his letters or other writings to the September massacres.

A member of no faction, Paine found himself closest to the moderate democratic republican Girondins, led by his friend from 1791, Jacques-Pierre Brissot de Warville. He was comfortable politically with their belief in property and the market and their confidence in reason as a guide to action. A further recommendation was that many of their leading figures spoke English. But he was as acquainted with the Jacobins, whose leaders shared a similar background to that of the Girondins but who had closer links with the lower classes and were, to that extent, more militant. Condorcet remained active, but Lafayette, to whom Paine had dedicated the second part of *Rights of Man*, had defected to the Austrians, fearing for his life following accusations of monarchist sympathies.

Paine attended the National Convention's first session on 21 September. Between the Girondins and the Jacobins (perched on higher seats with their allies and called 'The Mountain'), sat the uncommitted bulk of deputies, 'The Plain'. The Convention's first act was to abolish the monarchy, with Paine's wholehearted approval. But almost at once he discovered how out of place his sentiments might be. Georges-Jacques Danton demanded a purge of the judiciary, which he said was tainted by connection with the old regime. As Danton's words were translated, Paine stood and insisted that the people's rights were endangered if justice was not in the hands of men educated in the law. Danton's proposal was carried. On 25 September Paine's friend Nicholas de Bonneville published a *Letter of Thomas Paine to the People of France*. Already Paine's words had an almost quaintly idealistic ring amidst the growing bitterness. 'Be calm, let us punish by instructing, rather than by revenge. Let us begin a new era by a greatness of friendship, and hail the approach of union and success.'[2]

On 11 October the Convention appointed Paine, Condorcet and Brissot to an eight-strong committee to prepare a constitution. Madame Roland, whose salon was a Girondin meeting place, commented of Paine's appointment that she thought him 'better fitted to sow the seeds of popular commotion, than to lay the foundations or prepare the form of government'.[3] A lengthy drafting process now began as the political crisis heightened. Paine realised the shift in power from the Girondins towards the Jacobins, with the fate of Louis dominating the argument. At the end of the month he addressed the Convention, congratulating its members on creating a republic but warning against executing Louis. 'It is the kingly office, rather than the officer, that is destructive. This is not seen by everyone.'[4]

Outside the Convention Paine continued the easy, sociable ways to which he had grown accustomed in London, now the central figure of a cosmopolitan circle of revolutionaries in the British Club at White's Hotel. The members included Christie, whom Paine had become close friends with in Paris in 1789, and Joel Barlow, an American radical writer whom Paine had first met in London. This was Paine's atmosphere, idealistically discussing the theory and practice of revolution. Lord Fitzgerald, a former British soldier and member of the Irish House of Commons, convinced Paine, who had been elected to the membership of the Society of United Irishmen in Dublin, to appeal to the French to finance a fight for independence against Britain. Fitzgerald wrote of Paine to his mother, 'I cannot express how kind he is to me; there is a simplicity of man, a goodness of heart, and a strength of mind in him, that I never knew a man before possess.'[5] Fitzgerald was to die in the 1798 Irish rising.

The club held a banquet at White's Hotel on 18 November 1792 to celebrate the French victory over the Austrians at Jemappes a few days earlier. Among the 75 guests were Paine, Christie, Fitzgerald and possibly the English poet William Wordsworth. A British government spy reported that the party sang French revolutionary songs and drank 13 toasts, symbolising the American states that had broken from Britain. Paine and his friends declared their solidarity with the French people, sent greetings to the Society for Constitutional Information in London, and talked hopefully of a democratic union of France and Britain.

Through October and early November the Girondins, supported by Paine, had argued that Louis was insignificant, that his punishment would be an empty gesture. But on 15 November the Convention accepted repeated Jacobin demands for his trial. Five days later, incriminating papers were found in the former royal apartments showing Louis had conspired with the revolution's internal and external enemies. Paine described Louis to the

Convention as a 'weak and narrow-minded man, badly reared', but accepted Louis had to face justice. He appealed for compassion. 'He that would make his own liberty secure must guard even his enemy from oppression; for if he violates this duty he establishes a precedent that will reach to himself.'[6]

The trial for conspiracy against public liberty and safety opened in the Convention on 11 December, adjourned after Louis had undergone three hours questioning, and reconvened on 15 January 1793. Paine told the Convention his abhorrence of monarchy was well known, as was his compassion for the unfortunate, whether friend or enemy. He appealed for Louis to be spared execution and reminded the deputies of the aid Louis had given to the Americans in their struggle. 'Let then those United States be the guard and the asylum of Louis Capet. There, in the future, remote from the miseries and crimes of royalty, he may learn, from the constant presence of public prosperity, that the true system of government consists not in monarchs, but in fair, equal, and honourable representation.'[7] Paine persisted in his pleas, but by the evening of 17 January the deputies had sentenced Louis to death, by a majority of one. Two days later the Convention's clerk read a further address by Paine expressing his sorrow at the decision. The radical physician Jean Paul Marat, with whom Paine had clashed before, angrily interrupted, shouting that he had no right to give his opinion because as a Quaker he opposed capital punishment on principle. Paine replied that his view was based as much on public policy as on morality. Louis was guillotined in the Place de la Révolution on 21 January. Shortly before leaving England Paine had told a friend, 'If the French kill their king, it will be a signal for my departure, for I will not abide among sanguinary men.'[8] But Paine remained, exiled from England and, following France's declaration of war on Britain and Holland in February, unable to risk crossing the Atlantic for fear of interception by the Royal Navy.

The execution of Louis, combined with a nationwide conscription of men for the army, intensified counter-revolutionary resistance. The most serious was a rising in the Vendée in the west of the country. As inflation took hold, the increasingly influential Jacobins demanded price controls, something Paine had opposed since his experience of similar attempts in Philadelphia in 1779. At the suggestion of Rickman, who thought his friend was drinking too much, Paine moved to St Denis, a country retreat on the outskirts of Paris early in 1793. He later wrote fondly of feeding ducks and geese from the parlour window, eating oranges and apricots from the garden, and happy visits from Wollstonecraft, Barlow and his wife.

The draft constitution, presented to the Convention on 15 February, proved a disappointment and debate dragged on into May. Paine had based his initial draft on the 1776 Pennsylvania Constitution, with a unicameral legislature and a collective executive, both directly elected. Condorcet edited and drew together this and the work of the other committee members. Paine was unhappy with the result, which seemed to him to concentrate on domestic concerns, excluding the international revolution. He need not have worried. Events ensured the constitution never came into force.

Paine now became politically isolated and played little part in the Convention. As the war went badly for France and the economy weakened, dissatisfaction grew with the Girondins, particularly among the poor who had seen little benefit from the revolution. In April the 'Mountain' accused over 20 deputies of being counter-revolutionaries, Paine's friends among them though not, as yet, Paine himself. He wrote to Jefferson on 20 April 1793, 'Had this revolution been conducted consistently with its principles, there was once a good prospect of extending liberty through the greatest part of Europe; but I now relinquish that hope.'⁹ He said he had contemplated returning to the United States but his house in New Rochelle had burnt down and he had insufficient money to build another.

On 2 June the Jacobins ousted the Girondins, the *sans-culottes* demanding the arrest of all traitors to the Revolution. Danton warned Paine not to enter the Convention. Power now moved to the Committee of Public Safety, dominated by Robespierre. As the Reign of Terror began, Paine retired to St Denis, despairing and, as he later admitted, again drinking heavily, but also writing intensely. Robespierre and St Just presented a new constitution, which they claimed to be ordained by the God of Reason. In October the Convention was suspended and the daily toll of executions grew, including those of the Girondin leaders, of Paine's close collaborator Condorcet and of Marie-Antoinette, the former queen. Paine's Girondin friends sang the Marseillaise, the revolution's anthem, on their journey to the guillotine on 31 October.

A net was closing around Paine, under suspicion by the new regime as a foreigner and a recent protector of Louis. In October Robespierre noted to himself, 'Demand that Thomas Paine be decreed of accusation, for the interest of America, as well as of France.'¹⁰ On 27 December 1793 the Committee of General Security and Surveillance issued warrants for the arrest of Paine and his friend Anacharsis Clootz. Paine was detained at White's Hotel, where he had gone to celebrate the completion of his latest work, one on religion. He was taken to the Luxembourg Prison on 28 December. As he was arrested, Paine was able to ensure delivery of the manuscript of his book to Barlow.

THE AGE OF REASON

20

The book that Paine had been writing almost up to the moment of his arrest was *The Age of Reason, Being an Investigation of Truth and of Fabulous Theology*. This work secured Paine a reputation as an atheist, although his purpose in writing it had been the complete opposite. In 1803 he told Samuel Adams, his friend since 1776, 'The people of France were running headlong into atheism, and I had the work translated into their own language, to stop them in that career, and fix them to the first article of every man's creed, who has any creed at all – I believe in God.'[1] In 1776 Paine had described to John Adams his plans to set down his religious views in the latter part of his life. By mid-1793 Paine had a sense of urgency. 'I saw many of my most intimate friends destroyed; others daily carried to prison; and I had reason to believe, and had also some intimations given me, that the same danger was approaching myself.'[2]

Paine's argument was simple and eloquently put. The word of God could not be found in any holy book. He condemned all organised religion, which he said pretended a special mission from God, communicated by revelation to certain individuals, Moses, Christ, Mohammed. 'I do not believe in the creed professed by the Jewish church, by the Roman church, by the Greek church, by the Turkish church, by the Protestant church, nor by any church that I know of. My own mind is my own church.' All national churches, he said, were human inventions, established to terrify mankind and to monopolise power and profit. 'I believe in one God, and no more; and I hope for happiness beyond this life. I believe the equality of man, and I believe that religious duties consist in doing justice, loving mercy, and endeavouring to make our fellow-creatures happy.'[3]

He denounced the Old Testament, citing its unrelenting vindictiveness, debauchery and cruelty. 'It is a history of wickedness, that has served to corrupt and brutalize mankind; and, for my own part, I sincerely detest it, as I detest everything that is cruel'.[4] Christianity, he said, had emerged from a combination of the Old Testament and heathen mythology. Paine described Christ as 'a virtuous and an amiable man' who had preached a benevolent morality. Those who came after him had distorted his teaching to conjure up the ridiculous contradictions of New Testament Christianity. 'From whence could arise the solitary and strange conceit that the Almighty, who had millions of worlds equally dependent on his protection, should quit the care of all the rest, and come to die in our world, because, they say, one man and one woman had eaten an apple!'[5]

God, Paine the deist argued, was the first cause and could be apprehended by reason. The true revelation of God was creation itself. 'Do we want to contemplate his power? We see it in the immensity of the creation. Do we want to contemplate his wisdom? We see it in the unchangeable order by which the incomprehensible Whole is governed ... In fine, do we want to know what God is? Search not the book called the scripture, which any human hand might make, but the scripture called Creation.'[6]

Eighteenth-century deism was rooted in the Enlightenment and the intellectual influence of Newtonian physics, which suggested that nature was governed by laws that could be understood. Deists considered that God had created the universe but did not intervene through, for example, miracles. They believed that the nature of God was incomprehensible to the human mind, rejected revelation and organised religion and looked to reason as a guide to conduct. Washington, Jefferson, Franklin and Robespierre were deists, and before them Locke and Voltaire, though many kept up a façade of Christianity.

The first English edition of *The Age of Reason* appeared in February 1794 and was banned by the government, encouraging a flourishing underground market. In the United States, eight editions were published in 1794 alone, and translations circulated in France, Germany and even Hungary. Paine, once again, put forth in plain language what was already a commonplace among the educated, and, as with *Common Sense* and *Rights of Man*, he undermined deference and threatened tradition. Organised religion was a means of social control, accepted as such even by those who privately shared Paine's spiritual outlook. Paine called this a pious fraud. For crossing that line, and for offending those who did genuinely believe in revealed religion, he would be vilified for the remainder of his life.

But Paine's concern in January 1794 was how long that life would be. He later wrote, '[T]here was no time when I could think my life worth twenty-four hours, and my mind was made up to meet my fate.'[7] On his arrest, Paine was initially placed in a ground-floor cell ten feet by eight feet, with a chair, a mattress and a wooden box for his possessions. The Luxembourg held former aristocrats and British citizens. Paine described the prison keeper, Benoit, as a man of good heart who treated him well until he was dismissed and, it appears, guillotined.

On 20 January a group of Americans, including Barlow, went to the Convention to appeal for Paine's release. They were greeted with hissing. The Convention president, Vadier, who had signed the arrest warrant, said a few days later that although he recognised Paine's part in the American revolution, he was a native of England, a country with which France was now at war. In mid-February, Gouverneur Morris, the United States' representative in Paris, asked the French foreign minister to explain Paine's imprisonment. The minister said that Paine had renounced American citizenship by taking his Convention seat. Morris forwarded this letter to Paine and took no further action. He explained to Jefferson that pressing Paine's citizenship would be 'inexpedient and ineffectual' but if Paine stayed quiet he might escape 'the long suspended axe'. Morris could not refrain from adding that Paine 'amuses himself with publishing a pamphlet against Jesus Christ'. Morris told Jefferson in a subsequent letter that, even in the best of times, Paine 'had a larger share of every other sense than common sense, and lately the intemperate use of ardent spirits has, I am told, considerably impaired the small stock he originally possessed'.[8] Paine could not imagine the depth of hatred he had inspired in Morris.

Paine's life inside the Luxembourg fell into a similar pattern to that before his arrest. He wrote letters, including a coyly romantic correspondence with the wife of an English banker with whom he had become friends in Paris. He revised *The Age of Reason* and discussed religion and politics with Clootz, who had been arrested on the same day. Paine was popular with his fellow prisoners, one later writing, 'His cheerful philosophy under the certain expectation of death, his sensibility of heart, his brilliant powers of conversation, and his sportive vein of wit, rendered him a very general favourite with his companions of misfortune, who found a refuge from evil in the charms of his society.'[9] At the end of March, as Robespierre lashed out at the ultra-radicals and the remaining moderates alike, Clootz was taken to his death. Then Danton appeared at the Luxembourg and insisted on shaking Paine's hand. Danton was executed on 5 April.

As the strain and fear for his life took their toll, the 57-year-old Paine succumbed to a fever, probably typhus, in May and was transferred to a larger cell with three other prisoners. He was almost oblivious to what was happening about him but believed his sickness saved him from execution. On one night in July 160 people were taken from the Luxembourg to the guillotine. Paine believed he was to have been one of them. His companions had asked the guards' permission to leave their cell door open for ventilation. The door had then been chalked on the outside as a sign that they were to be taken to the guillotine with the next batch. But, Paine said, '[T]he mark was put on when the door was open, and flat against the wall, and thereby came on the inside when we shut it at night, and the destroying angel passed by it.'[10]

Robespierre fell from power on 17 July 1794 and was put to death the next day. Paine's recovery began. On 7 August he wrote to the Convention asking for his freedom, reminding the deputies that he was an American and calling Robespierre a hypocrite. There was no reaction. Paine's hopes of liberty rose when he heard that James Monroe had replaced Morris as ambassador. But Monroe moved slowly. Paine, in agony from a suppurating abscess in his side, suspected that even President Washington had abandoned him. Monroe told Paine in a letter that the president had given him no order to secure Paine's release, but Washington was possibly unaware of his predicament. While Paine waited, a pamphlet appeared in England reporting his execution and his final admission that he had 'written and spoken nothing but lies all my life'.[11]

On 2 November 1794 Monroe wrote to the Committee of General Security appealing for Paine's release on the grounds of his American citizenship, describing Paine as one of America's 'most distinguished patriots'. Two days later he was freed, having served ten months and nine days in the Luxembourg. Monroe invited Paine to stay at his house. Paine borrowed 250 French livres from Monroe and was still in his home a year later. Monroe wrote to a friend that it appeared his guest would remain 'till his death or departure for America, however remote either the one or the other event may be'.[12] Though weakened by recurring bouts of fever and suffering from the abscess in his side, Paine was soon in the Paris streets and coffee houses. Here he learnt from acquaintances that had begun to re-appear of the arrest of many of his radical friends in England, including Frost, Hardy, Horne Took and Walker. In May 1794 the British government had suspended *habeas corpus* and moved against the radical societies, forcing much of their activity under ground, heightening their radicalism but, in the midst of patriotic anti-French fervour, breaking their popular links.

In December 1794 Paine was invited to resume his seat in the Convention, with the promise of a pension for his literary contributions to the revolution, which he never received, and arrears of salary covering the period in the Luxembourg. Paine did not attend the Convention until 7 July 1795, when he contributed to the debate on a new constitution. He argued for universal suffrage (for men) in *Dissertation on First Principles of Government*, published simultaneously with his speech. Paine was politely heard by the Convention, but ignored. The constitution, which provided for indirect elections to two chambers, with executive power in the hands of a five-member Directory, came into force on 23 September 1795. Paine regarded it as a violation of the 1789 Declaration of the Rights of Man and the Citizen and he withdrew almost entirely from French politics.

In August 1795 Paine had completed the second part of *The Age of Reason*, a closer reading of the Bible convincing him the Old and New Testaments were worse than he had originally conceived: wicked religion and faulty history. He doubted anyone would believe a girl who said she had become pregnant by a ghost and that an angel had told her so. 'Why, then, are we to believe the same thing of another girl, whom we never saw, told by nobody knows who, nor when, nor where?'[13] He picked at the contradictions of the Gospels one by one, scorning the absurdities of Jesus's supposed resurrection. Christianity, he wrote, was derogatory to God, unedifying to man and repugnant to reason. 'Too absurd for belief, too impossible to convince, and too inconsistent for practice, it renders the heart torpid, or produces only atheists and fanatics. As an engine of power, it serves the purpose of despotism; and as a means of wealth, the avarice of priests; but so far as respects the good of man in general, it leads to nothing here or hereafter.'[14]

Paine's enemies would have seen divine intervention in the worsening of his illness a month after completion of *The Age of Reason*. In fact, Paine's relapse followed an over-enthusiastic celebration of the book's publication. The open wound in his side was now incurable and infection had spread to a rib, which was rotting. Monroe wrote to a friend in September 1795 that he expected Paine to last a month, two at the most. As Paine brooded on his life, his bitterness against Washington for having, as he believed, ignored his plight in the Luxembourg, burst out in a letter to James Madison. Monroe persuaded Paine not to dispatch the letter, but, despite an easing in his condition, the anger festered.

NOT CHARITY BUT A RIGHT

21

What finally provoked Paine into an open attack on Washington was a treaty between the United States and Britain that came into effect in February 1796. Jay's Treaty was intended to settle issues remaining from the war of independence but was widely unpopular in the United States, where it was seen as pro-British and anti-French. Paine, despite his disillusionment with the way in which the revolution had developed, remained a supporter of France. Indeed, in April 1796 he published *The Decline and Fall of the English System of Finance*, which the Directory, the five-strong executive, apparently paid him to write. The Foreign Affairs Ministry bought 1,000 copies, heartened by Paine's demonstration of the British economy's fragile foundations. Paine dedicated the royalties to the relief of those imprisoned for debt in Newgate, London.

The execution of Louis XVI in 1793 and war between France and Britain had marked out a division over foreign affairs in American politics. Washington, Adams and the Federalists feared what they saw as the revolution's excessive democracy and, sensitive to the interests of business, looked to Britain as a trading partner. Those who supported Jefferson and the Anti-Federalists (later the Democratic-Republicans) looked to France ideologically, reading their own commitment to a wider decentralised democracy into the French Revolution. Within a year of Jay's Treaty, France had broken off diplomatic relations with the United States.

The Federalists were one of the first political organisations in the United States, favouring strong central government, a broad interpretation of the Constitution, industrialisation, and a protective tariff. They were seen as pro-British. The Federalists' leading figures were John Adams, Alexander Hamilton, John Jay and John Marshall. Their Democratic-Republican opponents favoured weaker central government, with greater powers devolved to the states, agriculture and were pro-French. Their leading figures were Thomas Jefferson, James Madison and Aaron Burr.

Paine haunted coffee houses frequented by Americans in Paris denouncing the treaty, the Federalists and Washington. One of the Americans who had pleaded before the Convention for Paine's release from prison in 1794 remarked that Paine was 'like many other geniuses advanced in life, both vain and obstinate to an extreme degree'.[1] In the spring of 1796 Paine moved from Paris to Suresnes and poured his accumulated anger into a 70-page open *Letter to George Washington*. He finished work on 30 July 1796 and issued the letter in two sections, the first in October, the second as the American presidential elections approached in November, and the whole as a pamphlet in February 1797.

The first half was a critique of Jay's Treaty and its effects. Here he found some support among the Democratic-Republicans. But they were embarrassed by what followed, as Paine scathingly abused Morris, Adams and Washington. The Federalists, Paine said, were a party intent on pursuing their own interests rather than those of the United States. Washington was striving for personal aggrandisement and hoped, like Adams, to turn America into a monarchy (a charge dating back to arguments over the Constitution). That, Paine declared, was why Washington had not lifted a finger to free him from the Luxembourg. 'You folded your arms, forgot your friend, and became silent.' Paine had defended Washington as a commander when he came under criticism in 1778. He now mocked Washington's military competence. Paine concluded, 'And as to you, Sir, treacherous in private friendship (for so you have been to me, and that in the day of danger) and a hypocrite in public life, the world will be puzzled to decide whether you are an apostate or an impostor; whether you have abandoned good principles, or whether you ever had any.'[2]

Paine had suffered in the Luxembourg and had been neglected by the

American government, but much of what he said was unworthy of him. The election of Adams to the presidency in November appeared to vindicate Paine's Federalist enemies. Washington certainly read the letter, though he made no direct comment. But he did express his approval of an equally bitter article by the radical English journalist William Cobbett: 'Men will learn to express all that is base, malignant, treacherous, unnatural, and blasphemous, by one single monosyllable – Paine.'[3]

It seemed to be another Paine entirely who had, at the same time, been composing what would prove to be the last of his great pamphlets, *Agrarian Justice*. Paine was prompted into writing by the arrest in May 1796 of François Noël Babeuf, who was later executed for plotting in the 'Conspiracy of Equals' to overthrow the Directory and institute a state in which property would be equally divided. Paine, with his belief that private property and liberty ran hand-in-hand, disagreed with Babeuf. But equality had been a slogan of the revolution and Paine shared his view that this had yet to be achieved. *Agrarian Justice* was published first in France in 1796 and then in Britain and the United States in 1797.

Paine's opposition to monarchy and aristocracy had been based on his belief that government existed for the people, not the people for the government. The second part of *Rights of Man* and *Agrarian Justice* were a development of that view. Government should not only preserve order, it should be actively useful, and would be at its most useful by ending poverty through egalitarian redistribution. 'The great mass of the poor in all countries are become an hereditary race, and it is next to impossible for them to get out of that state themselves.' Combating poverty was not only morally right, it was wise politically. 'It is necessary as well for the protection of property as for the sake of justice and humanity, to form a system that, whilst it preserves one part of society from wretchedness, shall secure the other from depredation.'[4] Paine proposed a national fund, from which each person reaching the age of 21 would be given £15 sterling. From the age of 50, every person would be paid a pension of £10 a year. He argued that the land was the common property of the human race and that those without land had been, in effect, dispossessed. He did not blame the present owners and argued, against Babeuf, that it would be wrong to in turn dispossess them. He proposed a tax on land and personal property when passing from one owner to the next on death. This would build the national fund. He was, he said, no enemy of wealth. 'Though I care as little about riches as any man, I am a friend to riches because they are capable of good. I care not how affluent some may be, provided that none be miserable in consequence of it.' (Here was an echo of a point he had made 25 years previously in *The Case of the Officers of Excise*).

He went on, 'It is not charity but a right – not bounty but justice, that I am pleading for. The present state of civilization is as odious as it is unjust. It is the reverse of what it should be, and it is necessary that a revolution should be made in it. The contrast of affluence and wretchedness continually meeting and offending the eye, is like dead and living bodies chained together.'5 Though his hopes of 1776 and 1789 had been disappointed, Paine concluded with a rousing optimism. 'An army of principles will penetrate where an army of soldiers cannot – It will succeed where diplomatic management will fail – It is neither the Rhine, the Channel, nor the Ocean, that can arrest its progress – It will march on the horizon of the world, and it will conquer.'6 But moderate and, in modern terms, determinedly non-socialist as Paine's proposals were, they remained too egalitarian to be even considered by the governments of France, Britain and the United States.

Paine, now 60 years old, retained his interest in religion. He showed a growing emphasis on spirituality, partly under the influence of his friend, the radical journalist Nicolas de Bonneville. In January 1797 Paine and five families established the Society of Theophilanthropists (Friends of God and Man) in Paris, setting up a meeting place and library in the suburb of St Denis, aided by a government subsidy. The Society worshipped according to the deist principles Paine had set out in *The Age of Reason*, with no mythology and no priesthood. He wrote in a letter at the time, 'No man ought to make a living by religion. It is dishonest to do so. Religion is not an act that can be performed by proxy.'7 Paine gave the inaugural address, declaring that the Society's teaching would combine theological knowledge with scientific instruction.

But Paine's thoughts were turning again to the United States, though he remained ambivalent. He did not welcome Adams's election as president in 1796 and wrote to Madison in April 1797 that he was 'mortified at the fall of the American character. It was once respectable even to eminence; now it is despised; and did I not feel my own character as an individual, I should blush to call myself a citizen of America'. But with worsening relations between France and the United States, he feared re-arrest and stayed in Le Havre for several weeks, hesitating over whether to take ship to America. Returning to Paris he wrote to Madison that he would rather cross the Channel, '[A]nd should a revolution begin in England, I intend to be among them'.8

On his return from Le Havre Paine had been invited by Bonneville to stay with him, his wife and three sons (one named Thomas Paine Bonneville) in Paris for a week or two; he stayed for five years, renting a bedroom and study, which he called his workshop. The room overflowed with papers and the models of inventions. His habits were now ingrained: disordered rooms, rising late, scanning the newspapers. His grasp of the language had improved to the extent that he could read French as well as English political news. He wrote little but talked incessantly with friends at home and at the Irish Coffee House, mainly American and British exiles, many of his French associates having died in the Terror. Paine retained some contacts in government and could help with bureaucracy, securing passports or, in the case of Mary Wollstonecraft's brother, release from prison. Paine met the Irish republican Theobald Wolfe Tone in 1797, who remarked on Paine's vanity, adding, 'He drinks like a fish, a misfortune which I have known to befall other celebrated patriots. I am told, that the true time to see him to advantage is about ten at night, with a bottle of brandy and water before him, which I can very well conceive.'[9] Wolfe Tone was to commit suicide after being sentenced to death for his part in the French-backed 1798 Irish rising.

Paine joined a republican club following a shift to the constitutional monarchists in the April 1797 Assembly elections. The club was outlawed in the summer. On 4 September an army-backed coup replaced two members of the Directory with reliable republicans. The Directory imposed censorship and made calls for a return to monarchy punishable by death. Paine, either ignoring or failing to see the steps toward dictatorship, welcomed the coup in a pamphlet praised by the Directory. Paine asked, '[S]hall the Republic be destroyed by the darksome manoeuvres of a faction, or shall it be preserved by an exceptional act?'.[10] He hoped a militant republic would invade an England still unsteady after naval mutinies in April and May and provoke a revolution. Paine sent the Directory a copy of his newly-written *Observations on the Construction and Operation of Navies with a Plan for an Invasion of England and the Final Overthrow of the English Government.* Only General Napoleon Bonaparte, fresh from victories over the Austrians in Italy, showed interest in Paine's invasion plans, believing, as he told the Directory, that all military efforts should be directed at Britain. Bonaparte flattered Paine, telling him through Bonneville that he kept a copy of *Rights of Man* under his pillow and that a statue of gold should be erected in his honour in every city in the universe. British intelligence agents in Paris reported to London that if a French invasion succeeded, Ireland, Scotland and England would become republics, with Paine playing a prominent part in the English revolutionary government. Paine's view of Bonaparte altered when, on 9/10 November 1799, the Directory was overthrown and replaced by three Consuls, including Bonaparte, who emerged as dictator. At a banquet at which both were present, Bonaparte looked over at Paine and said, 'The English are alike in every country – they are all rascals.' Paine remarked at another dinner that Napoleon was, '[T]he greatest butcher of liberty, the greatest monster that nature ever spewed.'[11] Paine's friend Bonneville was later imprisoned and his newspaper outlawed for comparing Bonaparte with Cromwell.

In November 1800 Thomas Jefferson was elected President of the United States. Paine was determined to return, hoping for a welcome now that his friend had replaced the hated Adams. Paine told the English radical Henry Redhead Yorke that France was not a republic, that the people were worse off than slaves. 'I know of no Republic in the world except America, which is the only country for such men as you and I ... I have done with Europe, and its slavish politics.'[12] In March 1801 Jefferson, true to their friendship though aware from the election campaign of the embarrassment any connection with Paine's religious views could ignite, offered Paine passage home in an American warship. Paine declined but ensured Jefferson's offer appeared in the French press. When the story was repeated in America, Jefferson's Federalist opponents used it against him.

In March 1802 France and Britain temporarily made peace in the Treaty of Amiens, so Paine felt safe to cross the Atlantic. Madame Bonneville and her children were to follow and be joined by Bonneville himself when he was able to leave France. An English visitor in the weeks before Paine left remarked on his altered appearance. 'Time seemed to have made dreadful ravages over his whole frame, and a settled melancholy was visible on his countenance.'[13] An American was more direct. 'Drinking spirits has made his entire face as red as fire and his habits of life have rendered him so neglectful in his person that he is generally the most abominably dirty being upon the face of the earth.' But even she was moved by his charm. 'In spite of his surprising ugliness, the expression of his countenance is luminous, his manners easy and benevolent, and his conversation remarkably entertaining.'[14] Assisted by his loyal friend Rickman, Paine left Paris for Le Havre on 1 September 1802.

I CARE NOT A STRAW

22

Paine landed at Baltimore on 30 October 1802, weighed down with cases of papers and the bridge models that had accompanied him everywhere. He had been out of the United States for 15 years and was in many ways a figure from the past. But he had not been forgotten. Even before his arrival a Federalist newspaper in Boston described the 65-year-old Paine as 'a lying, drunken, brutal infidel, who rejoices in the opportunity of basking and wallowing in the confusion, devastation, bloodshed, rapine and murder, in which his soul delights'.[1]

The Federalists connected Paine with the excesses of the French Revolution, even though he had risked his life opposing the execution of Louis XVI and what followed. There were other reasons for their enmity: the *Letter to George Washington* and *The Age of Reason*. Even the Democratic-Republicans, who might be thought to share Paine's politics, stood back from him when Jefferson's religious views, and his association with Paine, became an issue in the 1800 presidential election. Jefferson had, despite his own deism, depended on Baptist, Methodist and Presbyterian votes.

Paine was sanguine about his reception, writing to Rickman that he could have 'no idea of the agitation which my arrival occasioned. From New Hampshire to Georgia (an extent of 1,500 miles), every newspaper was filled with applause or abuse'.[2] Paine's humour had not left him. At a tavern on the evening of his arrival he entertained his supporters with a poem he had written against himself, 'On a Long Nosed Friend'. The Philadelphia *Aurora* reported that Paine dressed plainly, like a farmer, but that his clothes bore the marks of the snuff he used profusely. Paine travelled down to Washington, then called Federal City, and was able to find a hotel willing to accommodate him only by using an assumed name. He dined with Jefferson, though as a private rather than an official guest.

Paine soon embroiled himself in domestic politics, writing a series of open letters *To the Citizens of the United States*. In the first, published on 15 November 1802, he attacked the Federalists, despite his proclaimed aversion to indulging in party politics. The Federalists, he said, saw government as 'a profitable monopoly, and the people as hereditary property'.[3] A week later he abused Adams, saying that his destiny was to 'begin with hypocrisy, proceed with arrogance, and finish in contempt'. Adams, he said, reverting to old accusations that the pro-British Federalists planned to install a monarchy, had a head 'as full of kings, queens and knaves, as a pack of cards'.[4] Jefferson refused entreaties from his supporters to quiet Paine, but began to keep his distance. The invitations and discussions ceased, though the two continued to exchange letters. Their politics had moved apart, though Paine seemed not to be aware of it. His social security proposals in *Rights of Man* and *Agrarian Justice* implied something more than the minimal state that he and Jefferson had once agreed on. When Paine wrote to Jefferson on 25 December 1802 to suggest that the United States should buy the Louisiana territory, lately ceded by Spain to France, Jefferson replied that matters were already in hand. He had thought it unwise to share his thoughts with Paine. In May 1803 the United States paid $15 million for Louisiana and doubled the size of the country.

In February 1803 Paine left for Philadelphia. But even here, the scene of his greatest triumph, his religious views had shattered long-standing friendships. Paine's supporters held celebratory banquets, but Rush, who had given *Common Sense* its title, refused to meet him, angered by what he saw as his blasphemies. Priestley, Paine's supporter in England in the early 1790s, shared Rush's opinion. In November 1802 Samuel Adams, a close comrade in 1776, told Paine of the disappointment he had felt when Paine had turned to a defence of religious infidelity. Paine, hurt at this misunderstanding of his intentions, replied early in 1803. 'Our relation to each other in this World is as Men, and the Man who is a friend to Man and to his rights, let his religious opinions be what they may, is a good citizen, to whom I can give, as I ought to do, and as every other ought, the right hand of fellowship, and to none with more hearty good will, my dear friend, than to you.'[5]

Paine left his bridge models at a museum in Philadelphia and moved on to Colonel Kirkbride's house in Bordentown, where Madame Bonneville and her three sons were waiting to greet him on 24 February. Paine was accepted here, despite his infidel reputation, and spent most evenings in a local tavern enthralling admirers with his well-stocked repertoire of stories. But on 2 March a coach driver at Trenton (where American soldiers inspired by the first of the *Crisis Papers* had overwhelmed the Hessian mercenaries in 1777) refused to carry him to New York City and a hostile crowd jostled him. However, in New York itself Paine was cheered by immigrants from Britain, many of whom knew his *Rights of Man*, and feted at welcoming rallies.

In the autumn Paine stayed at his sparsely furnished farm at New Rochelle but, tiring of country life, he returned in January 1804 to New York City, where he was followed by the financially dependent Madame Bonneville and her sons. By the spring he had returned to New Rochelle, writing to Jefferson, 'I live upon tea, milk, fruit pies, plain dumplings, and a piece of meat when I can get it.'[6] In the summer he sold 60 acres, raising $4,000 to clear his debts. Paine continued writing on religion, producing 17 essays for a deist journal, *The Prospect*, many under pen names to spare Jefferson embarrassment in an election year. With Jefferson's victory over the Federalists in November, Paine declared there was no more to be said. 'I shall do as I did after the war, remain a quiet spectator and attend now to my own affairs.'[7] What he did have to say in occasional journalism often harked back to 1776 and seemed irrelevant to the new generation of Americans.

Paine's concern, as throughout his life, continued to be his hand-to-mouth existence. Plans to publish his collected writings came to nothing. In September 1805 he wrote to Jefferson asking the government to grant him more land. Returning to New York at the invitation of a supporter, Paine stayed five months, much of which he spent with workers who treated him with respect but encouraged his drinking, up to a quart of brandy an evening. On 25 July 1805 he fell down a flight of stairs and was confined to bed until October. A visitor, exasperated during a heated argument about religion confronted Paine with what his life had become. 'Mr Paine, here you sit, in an obscure, uncomfortable dwelling, powdered with snuff and stupefied with brandy; you, who were once the companion of Washington, Jay, and Hamilton, are now deserted by every good man; and even respectable deists cross the streets to avoid you.' Paine pulled himself up and fixed the visitor with his gaze. 'I care not a straw for the opinions of the world.'[8]

A worse humiliation came in November 1805 for the man who had inspired the birth of and had given a name to the United States. Paine travelled to New Rochelle to vote in Congressional and state elections. When he handed in his ballots the superintendent refused to accept them on the grounds that he was not an American citizen. When Paine argued, the officer said that neither President Washington nor Gouverneur Morris had recognised him as such when he was in prison. Paine took the matter to court, circulating his friends, including Monroe and Vice-President Clinton, for testimonials, but lost the case.

Paine's life became increasingly isolated as he moved from house to house in New York City, his health deteriorating. He stayed with a painter, John Wesley Jarvis (who was to produce his death mask) and then took rooms with a sympathetic baker on the edge of the city. He had few visitors. Paine wrote to Bonneville in France asking why he could not come to America (Napoleon was preventing him) and asked his friend Barlow in Paris why he never heard from him. In January 1808 Paine moved to the worst possible environment, a tavern. He wrote to Congress asking for reimbursement of the costs of his mission to France in 1781. 'I have been a volunteer to the world for thirty years without taking profits from anything I have published in America or in Europe.'[9] Only a firm rebuff from Jefferson prevented him pressing his case any further. In July 1808 Paine sold his house and meadow at Bordentown for $800 and moved in with friends at Greenwich, a village north of New York City.

As his health worsened, Paine lost the use of his legs, passing the days propped at a table, papers and books scattered around him. His companions often found him sitting in tears and, though he showed no self-pity, he was in an anguish of disappointment and loneliness. His condition weakened through the autumn of 1808 and Paine needed constant attention.

On 18 January 1809 Paine wrote his will, the last of a number he had composed. There were bequests to his literary executors and his friend Rickman from the sale of his property. What remained was to go to Madame Bonneville in trust for her children's education. Paine concluded the document. 'I have lived an honest and useful life to mankind; my time has been spent in doing good, and I die in perfect composure and resignation to the will of my Creator, God.'[10] But he lived on, in constant pain from ulcerous wounds on his feet, bed sores and the swelling abdomen of dropsy.

Paine's remaining hope was to be buried in a Quaker cemetery, in deference perhaps to his father. On 19 March 1809 he asked a Quaker neighbour whether this would be possible. The congregation refused, concerned, they said, that his friends would want to erect a monument to him, which was contrary to their rules. With no prospect of recovery, Paine was carried in a chair to a house that Madame Bonneville had rented nearby to care for him in his final days. There was no weakening of his principles and his determination to defend them. Two clergymen pushed their way into the house and called on him to repent. Paine dismissed them. 'Let me have none of your Popish stuff. Get away with you.' When a doctor asked him if he wished to believe that Jesus was the son of God, Paine replied, loudly, 'I have no wish to believe on that subject.'[11]

Paine's final words were to Madame Bonneville, replying 'Oh, yes' when she asked whether he was happy with the care he had received. He died next morning, 8 June 1809, and was taken for burial on his farm at New Rochelle the following day. Madame Bonneville, her children, two black Americans, a Quaker neighbour, Paine's two literary executors, and a carriage of Irishmen, made the 25-mile journey from Greenwich to the farm. Madame Bonneville stood at the foot of Paine's grave, one of her sons facing her. 'Oh! Mr Paine! My son stands here as testimony of the gratitude of America, and I, for France!'[12] The press barely noticed Paine's passing and there was no word from any of the public figures who remained from 1776. But after Paine's death children sang a rhyme, probably composed by one of his enemies:

> 'Poor Tom Paine! There he lies,
> Nobody laughs and nobody cries.
> Where he has gone or how he fares,
> Nobody knows and nobody cares.'

In 1819 William Cobbett, the English journalist who had attacked Paine in 1796 but who had become a leading admirer, went to New Rochelle with two companions and dug up Paine's bones to give them what he believed would be a proper burial in England. The bones disappeared mysteriously, either lost at sea or mislaid following Cobbett's own death in 1835.

ENDNOTES

Introduction

1. Thomas Paine, *Common Sense*, in *Rights of Man, Common Sense and Other Political Writings*, ed Mark Philp (Oxford University Press, Oxford: 1998) p 35, hereafter Paine, *Common Sense*.
2. Quoted in Christopher Hill, *The World Turned Upside Down: Radical Ideas during the English Revolution* (Penguin Books, Harmondsworth: 1974) p 366.

1. A moral education

1. Thomas Paine, *Rights of Man*, in *Rights of Man, Common Sense and Other Political Writings*, ed Mark Philp (Oxford University Press, Oxford: 1998) p 272, hereafter Paine, *Rights of Man*.
2. Thomas Paine, *The Age of Reason, Being an Investigation of True and Fabulous Theology*, ed Moncure Daniel Conway (Dover Publications, Mineola: 2004) p 65, hereafter Paine, *The Age of Reason*.

3. Quoted in Moncure Daniel Conway, *The Life of Thomas Paine with a history of his literary, political and religious career in America, France, and England*, ed Hypatia Bradlaugh Bonner (Watts, London: 1909), p 5.
4. Conway, *Life of Thomas Paine*, p 2.
5. Paine, *Rights of Man*, p 271.
6. Paine, *The Age of Reason*, pp 62–3, 66.
7. John Keane, *Tom Paine: A Political Life* (Bloomsbury, London: 1995) p 20.
8. Paine, *Common Sense*, p 5.
9. Paine, *The Age of Reason*, p 57.

2. Enlightenment

1. Paine, *Rights of Man*, p 272.
2. Paine, *Rights of Man*, p 272.
3. Paine, *Common Sense*, p 39.
4. Keane, *Tom Paine: A Political Life*, p 52; Samuel Edwards, *Rebel! A Biography of Thomas Paine* (New York and London: 1974) p 22.

3. Strictness of duty

1. Quoted in Jack Fruchtman Jr, *Thomas Paine: Apostle of Freedom* (Four Walls Eight Windows, New York and London: 1994) p 35.
2. Thomas Paine, *The American Crisis 1*, in *Rights of Man, Common Sense and Other Political Writings*, ed Mark Philp (Oxford University Press, Oxford: 1998) p 69, hereafter Paine, *Crisis 1*.
3. Eric Foner, *Tom Paine and Revolutionary America* (Oxford University Press, Oxford and New York: 1976) p 14.
4. Keane, *Tom Paine: A Political Life*, p 69.

4. Ingenious young man

1. Keane, *Tom Paine: A Political Life*, p 71.
2. Fruchtman, *Thomas Paine: Apostle of Freedom*, p 34.
3. Foner, *Tom Paine and Revolutionary America*, pp 14–15; Keane, *Tom Paine: A Political Life*, p 73.
4. Conway, *Life of Thomas Paine*, p 13.
5. Paine, 'Reflections on Unhappy Marriages', quoted in Conway, *Life of Thomas Paine*, p 18.
6. David Freeman Hawke, *Paine* (W W Norton, New York and London: 1992) p 22.

5. The climate of America

1. Gordon S Wood, *The American Revolution: A History* (Phoenix paperback edition, London: 2005) p 37.
2. Wood, *The American Revolution: A History*, p 51.
3. Thomas Paine, *The Magazine in America*, quoted in Fruchtman, *Thomas Paine: Apostle of Freedom*, p 44.
4. Fruchtman, *Thomas Paine: Apostle of Freedom*, p 39.

6. Thus far a Quaker

1. Paine, 'African Slavery in America', quoted in Foner, *Tom Paine and Revolutionary America*, p 73.
2. Paine, 'Reflections on Unhappy Marriages', quoted in Fruchtman, *Thomas Paine: Apostle of Freedom*, p 37.
3. Paine, 'An Occasional Letter on the Female Sex', quoted in Conway, *Life of Thomas Paine*, p 19.
4. Paine, *Rights of Man*, pp 28–9.
5. Paine, 'Reflections on Titles', quoted in Conway, *Life of Thomas Paine*, p 18.
6. Paine, 'Thoughts on Defensive War', quoted in Keane, *Tom Paine: A Political Life*, p 102.

7. To begin the world over again

1. Paine, *Common Sense*, pp 3, 5, 7.
2. Paine, *Common Sense*, pp 9, 11, 34.
3. Paine, *Common Sense*, p 10.
4. Paine, *Common Sense*, pp 15, 16, 19.
5. Paine, *Common Sense*, pp 20, 26, 27, 29.
6. Paine, *Rights of Man*, p 210.
7. Paine, *Common Sense*, pp 33, 34.
8. Paine, *Common Sense*, pp 21, 24.
9. Paine, *Common Sense*, p 35.

8. A statue of gold

1. Thomas Paine, *The American Crisis 13*, in *Rights of Man, Common Sense and Other Political Writings*, ed Mark Philp (Oxford University Press, Oxford: 1998) p 77, hereafter Paine, *Crisis 13*.
2. David McCullough, *John Adams* (Simon and Schuster, New York: 2001) p 96; Keane, *Tom Paine: A Political Life*, p 128; Foner, *Tom Paine and Revolutionary America*, p 86.
3. Paine, *Rights of Man*, p 272.

4. McCullough, *John Adams*, p 97; Fruchtman, *Thomas Paine: Apostle of Freedom*, p 78.
5. Fruchtman, *Thomas Paine: Apostle of Freedom*, p 60.
6. Paine, *Common Sense*, pp 55–6.
7. Keane, *Tom Paine: A Political Life*, p 128.

9. The American crisis
1. Keane, *Tom Paine: A Political Life*, p 560.
2. Hawke, *Paine*, p 59.
3. Paine, *Crisis 1*, p 66.
4. Paine, *Crisis 1*, p 63.
5. Paine, *Crisis 1*, pp 66–7, 69.
6. Fruchtman, *Thomas Paine: Apostle of Freedom*, pp 457–8.
7. Foner, *Tom Paine and Revolutionary America*, p 140.

10. Stranger without connections
1. Keane, *Tom Paine: A Political Life*, p 157.
2. Keane, *Tom Paine: A Political Life*, p 167; Fruchtman, *Thomas Paine: Apostle of Freedom*, p 103.
3. Foner, *Tom Paine and Revolutionary America*, p 140; Fruchtman, *Thomas Paine: Apostle of Freedom*, p 108.

11. Neither the place nor the people
1. Paine, *Rights of Man*, p 273.
2. Keane, *Tom Paine: A Political Life*, p 185.
3. Foner, *Tom Paine and Revolutionary America*, p 173.
4. Hawke, *Paine*, p 101.
5. Conway, *Life of Thomas Paine*, p 63.
6. Keane, *Tom Paine: A Political Life*, p 200.

12. Never was a man less beloved
1. Paine, *Rights of Man*, p 273; Conway, *Life of Thomas Paine*, p 70.
2. Keane, *Tom Paine: A Political Life*, pp 205–6.
3. Hawke, *Paine*, p 114.
4. Fruchtman, *Thomas Paine: Apostle of Freedom*, p 133.
5. Conway, *Life of Thomas Paine*, p 73.

13. A great nation
1. Conway, *Life of Thomas Paine*, p 75.
2. Keane, *Tom Paine: A Political Life*, p 229.

3. Hawke, *Paine*, p 130.
4. Foner, *Tom Paine and Revolutionary America*, p 191.
5. Paine, *Crisis 13*, pp 72, 73, 78.
6. Fruchtman, *Thomas Paine: Apostle of Freedom*, pp 150–1.
7. Hawke, *Paine*, p 143.
8. Conway, *Life of Thomas Paine*, pp 84–5.

14. Bridges and candles
1. Conway, *Life of Thomas Paine*, p 86.
2. Foner, *Tom Paine and Revolutionary America*, p 204.
3. Conway, *Life of Thomas Paine*, p 87.
4. Conway, *Life of Thomas Paine*, p 91.
5. Conway, *Life of Thomas Paine*, p 102.
6. Hawke, *Paine*, p 174.
7. Fruchtman, *Thomas Paine: Apostle of Freedom*, p 185.
8. Conway, *Life of Thomas Paine*, p 97.
9. Conway, *Life of Thomas Paine*, p 102.
10. Letter to Washington, 21 July 1791, quoted in Conway, *Life of Thomas Paine*, p 131.

15. Reflections on the Revolution
1. Hawke, *Paine*, pp 198–9.
2. Keane, *Tom Paine: A Political Life*, p 281.
3. Conway, *Life of Thomas Paine*, p 110.
4. Fruchtman, *Thomas Paine: Apostle of Freedom*, p 211.
5. Conway, *Life of Thomas Paine*, p 112.
6. Hawke, *Paine*, p 211.
7. Quoted in Frank Prochaska, *The Republic of Britain 1760 to 2000* (Allen Lane, The Penguin Press, London: 2000) p 14.

16. *Rights of Man*, Part One
1. Paine, *Rights of Man*, p 100.
2. Paine, *Rights of Man*, pp 100–1, 107.
3. Paine, *Rights of Man*, p 102.
4. Paine, *Rights of Man*, pp 92, 117.
5. Paine, *Rights of Man*, p 123.
6. Paine, *Rights of Man*, pp 134, 169, 194.
7. Paine, *Rights of Man*, p 197.
8. Prochaska, *The Republic of Britain 1760 to 2000*, p 15.
9. Fruchtman, *Thomas Paine: Apostle of Freedom*, p 231.

10.Hawke, *Paine*, p 226.

11. Keane, *Tom Paine: A Political Life*, p 313.

17. England is not yet free

1. Conway, *Life of Thomas Paine*, p 128.
2. Fruchtman, *Thomas Paine: Apostle of Freedom*, p 238.
3. Hawke, *Paine*, p 229.
4. Keane, *Tom Paine: A Political Life*, p 319.
5. Conway, *Life of Thomas Paine*, p 131.
6. Conway, *Life of Thomas Paine*, p 130.
7. Hawke, *Paine*, p 233.
8. Conway, *Life of Thomas Paine*, p 132.
9. Hawke, *Paine*, p 244.

18. *Rights of Man*, Part Two

1. Paine, *Rights of Man*, p 234.
2. Paine, *Rights of Man*, pp 224, 258.
3. Paine, *Rights of Man*, pp 236, 251.
4. Paine, *Rights of Man*, p 317.
5. Paine, *Rights of Man*, pp 295, 296.
6. Paine, *Rights of Man*, p 295.
7. Paine, *Rights of Man*, pp 300–1.
8. Paine, *Rights of Man*, pp 215–16.
9. Conway, *Life of Thomas Paine*, p 139.
10.Hawke, *Paine*, p 248.
11. E P Thompson, *The Making of the English Working Class* (Penguin Books, Harmondsworth: 1977 paperback edition) p 121.
12. Thomas Paine, *Letter Addressed to the Addressers, On the Late Proclamation*, in *Rights of Man, Common Sense and Other Political Writings*, ed Mark Philp (Oxford University Press, Oxford: 1998) p 376.
13. Fruchtman, *Thomas Paine: Apostle of Freedom*, p 267.
14.Keane, *Tom Paine: A Political Life*, p 343.
15. Conway, *Life of Thomas Paine*, p 152.
16.Hawke, *Paine*, p 270.

19. Among sanguinary men

1. Fruchtman, *Thomas Paine: Apostle of Freedom*, p 279.
2. Fruchtman, *Thomas Paine: Apostle of Freedom*, p 280.
3. Hawke, *Paine*, pp 262–3.
4. Conway, *Life of Thomas Paine*, p 146.

5. Fruchtman, *Thomas Paine: Apostle of Freedom*, p 285.
6. Keane, *Tom Paine: A Political Life*, p 362.
7. Conway, *Life of Thomas Paine*, p 157.
8. Hawke, *Paine*, p 277.
9. Foner, *Tom Paine and Revolutionary America*, p 242.
10. Paine, *The Age of Reason*, p 86.

20. *The Age of Reason*
1. Paine, *The Age of Reason*, p 205.
2. Paine, *The Age of Reason*, p 85.
3. Paine, *The Age of Reason*, pp 21–2.
4. Paine, *The Age of Reason*, p 34.
5. Paine, *The Age of Reason*, p 73.
6. Paine, *The Age of Reason*, p 46.
7. Fruchtman, *Thomas Paine: Apostle of Freedom*, p 322.
8. Conway, *Life of Thomas Paine*, pp 202–3.
9. Hawke, *Paine*, p 301.
10. Conway, *Life of Thomas Paine*, pp 208–9.
11. Fruchtman, *Thomas Paine: Apostle of Freedom*, p 331.
12. Hawke, *Paine*, p 307.
13. Paine, *The Age of Reason*, p 157.
14. Paine, *The Age of Reason*, p 190.

21. Not charity but a right
1. Hawke, *Paine*, p 319.
2. Fruchtman, *Thomas Paine: Apostle of Freedom*, p 352.
3. Hawke, *Paine*, p 321.
4. Thomas Paine, *Agrarian Justice*, in *Rights of Man, Common Sense and Other Political Writings*, ed Mark Philp (Oxford University Press, Oxford: 1998) pp 426–7, 429, hereafter Paine, *Agrarian Justice*.
5. Paine, *Agrarian Justice*, p 425.
6. Paine, *Agrarian Justice*, p 430.
7. Conway, *Life of Thomas Paine*, p 260.
8. Hawke, *Paine*, pp 323–4.
9. Keane, *Tom Paine: A Political Life*, p 437.
10. Hawke, *Paine*, p 327.
11. Hawke, *Paine*, p 339.
12. Conway, *Life of Thomas Paine*, p 277.
13. Conway, *Life of Thomas Paine*, p 277.
14. Hawke, *Paine*, pp 346–7.

22. I care not a straw

1. Keane, *Tom Paine: A Political Life*, p 456.
2. Fruchtman, *Thomas Paine: Apostle of Freedom*, p 397.
3. Hawke, *Paine*, p 357.
4. Fruchtman, *Thomas Paine: Apostle of Freedom*, pp 398–9.
5. Paine, *The Age of Reason*, p 208.
6. Fruchtman, *Thomas Paine: Apostle of Freedom*, p 415.
7. Hawke, *Paine*, p 375.
8. Keane, *Tom Paine: A Political Life*, p 520.
9. Fruchtman, *Thomas Paine: Apostle of Freedom*, p 423.
10. Hawke, *Paine*, p 395.
11. Hawke, *Paine*, p 397.
12. Conway, *Life of Thomas Paine*, p 323.

FURTHER READING

The most extensive collection of Paine's journalism, books and letters is *The Complete Writings of Thomas Paine*, edited by Philip S Foner (Citadel Press, New York: 1945). This is not easily available to the general reader and for Paine's main works I have cited the more accessible Thomas Paine, *Rights of Man, Common Sense and Other Political Writings*, edited by Mark Philp (Oxford University Press, Oxford and New York: 1998) and Thomas Paine, *The Age of Reason, Being an Investigation of True and Fabulous Theology*, edited by Moncure Daniel Conway (Dover Publications, Mineola: 2004). There are many other editions of Paine's major writings.

The most recent substantial biographies of Paine are Jack Fruchtman Jr, *Thomas Paine: Apostle of Freedom* (Four Walls Eight Windows, New York and London: 1994), John Keane, *Tom Paine: A Political Life* (Bloomsbury, London: 1995) and David Freeman Hawke, *Paine* (W W Norton, New York and London: 1992 paperback edition). Keane is detailed, definitive and undoubtedly supersedes any previous study, but Fruchtman and Hawke are more readable. While not strictly a biography, Eric Foner, *Tom Paine and*

Revolutionary America (Oxford University Press, Oxford and New York: 1976) should be consulted, not least for Foner's superbly evocative and politically astute description of the Philadelphia that Paine knew. *These Are The Times, A Life of Thomas Paine* (Spokesman, Nottingham: 2005) is an excellent screenplay by Trevor Griffiths for a long-awaited film.

Mark Philp's short study, *Paine* (Oxford University Press, Oxford and New York: 1989), has an overview of his subject's thought. Other useful works on Paine's ideas are Gregory Claeys, *Thomas Paine: Social and Political Thought* (Unwin Hyman, London and Boston: 1989) and Jack Fruchtman Jr, *Thomas Paine and the Religion of Nature* (Johns Hopkins University Press, Baltimore: 1993). Gareth Stedman Jones's *An End to Poverty? A Historical Debate* (Profile Books, London: 2004) describes and analyses the advanced ideas of Paine and his friend Condorcet about eradicating poverty.

On the political and cultural environment in which Paine acted, see Isaac Kramnick, *Republicanism and Bourgeois Radicalism: Political Ideology in late Eighteenth-Century England and America* (Cornell University Press, Ithaca and London: 1990) and Roy Porter, *Enlightenment: Britain and the Creation of the Modern World* (Penguin, Harmondsworth: 2001 paperback edition), published in the United States as *The Creation of the Modern World: The Untold Story of the British Enlightenment* (Norton, New York: 2000). Robert A Ferguson covers the American context in *The American Enlightenment 1750-1820* (Harvard University Press, Cambridge Mass.: 1997).

For a concise but comprehensive study of the struggle for an independent United States, Gordon S Wood, *The American Revolution. A History* (Phoenix paperback edition, London: 2005) is good value. On the background against which Paine's *Common Sense* met with such acclaim, see Pauline Maier, *From Resistance to Revolution: Colonial Radicals and the Development of American Opposition to Britain* (Vintage, New York: 1972). Among other useful works are Theodore Draper, *A Struggle for Power. The American Revolution* (Vintage, New York and London: 1997) and Gordon S Wood, *The Radicalism of the American Revolution: How a Revolution Transformed a Monarchical Society into a Democratic One Unlike Any That Had Ever Existed* (Knopf, New York: 1992). See also Francis D Cogliano, *Revolutionary America 1763-1815: A Political History* (Routledge, London: 2000) and Robert Middlekauf, *The Glorious Cause: The American Revolution, 1763-1789* (Oxford University Press, Oxford and New York: 1982).

The impact of events in the American colonies on British politics is covered in Lee Ward, *The Politics of Liberty in England and Revolutionary America* (Cambridge University Press, Cambridge: 2004), Keith Perry, *British Politics and the American Revolution* (Macmillan Education, Basingstoke: 1990), and Colin Bonwick, *English Radicals and the American Revolution* (University of North Carolina Press, Chapel Hill: 1977).

Linda Colley, *Britons: Forging the Nation 1707-1837* (Yale University Press, London and New Haven: 1992, and subsequent paperback editions) is a bracing analysis of the invention of the Britain into which Paine was born, matured, and which he struggled to re-invent. E P Thomson's *The Making of the English Working Class* (Gollancz, London: 1963, and subsequent paperback editions) has much to say about Paine and his influence on radical struggles in Britain. Frank Prochaska has interesting observations on the politics of Paine and his contemporaries in his history of anti-monarchism *The Republic of Britain 1760 to 2000* (Allen Lane; The Penguin Press, London: 2000). For the life of the monarch whom Paine served as an excise officer and then sought to make redundant, see John Brooke, *George III* (Constable, London: 1985).

William Doyle, *The Oxford History of the French Revolution* (Oxford University Press, Oxford: 2nd edition 2003) is a useful place to start for events in France. His *The Origins of the French Revolution* (Oxford University Press, Oxford and New York: 3rd edition 1999) is also worth study. Simon Schama's *Citizens: A Chronicle of the French Revolution* (Viking, London and New York: 1989) is a vivid and energetic narrative. Among other relatively recent contributions are J R Censer and L Hunt, *Liberty, Equality and Fraternity: Exploring the French Revolution* (Pennsylvania State University Press, University Park: 2001), G Kates (ed), *The French Revolution: Recent Debates and New Controversies* (Routledge, London and New York: 1997), A Forrest, *The French Revolution* (Blackwell, Oxford and Cambridge Mass.: 1995) and T C W Blanning (ed), *The Rise and Fall of the French Revolution* (Chicago University Press, Chicago and London: 1996). For a biography of the French king whom Paine tried to save from execution, see John Hardman, *Louis XVI: The Silent King* (Oxford University Press, London and New York: 2000).

Paine's main concern after 1789 was how the French Revolution would reverberate in Britain. Iain Hampsher-Monk's *The Impact of the French Revolution* (Cambridge University Press, Cambridge: 2005) has valuable insights into this and into the writings of Paine, his adversary Burke, Wollstonecraft and less well known contemporaries. Among other useful contributions are C Emsley, *Britain and the French Revolution* (Longman, New York: 2000), Mark Philp (ed), *The French Revolution and British Popular Politics* (Cambridge University Press, Cambridge: 1991), H T Dickinson (ed), *Britain and the French Revolution 1789-1815* (Macmillan, Basingstoke: 1989) and his *British Radicalism and the French Revolution 1789-1815* (Blackwell, Oxford:

1985). See also S Deane, *The French Revolution and Enlightenment in England 1789-1832* (Harvard University Press, Cambridge Mass.: 1988).

INDEX

A

Adams, John 29, 34, 35–6, 41, 62, 72, 90, 96, 97, 101
Adams, Samuel 27, 103
Aitken, Robert 21, 27, 34
Alliance (gunboat) 52
American Revolution, the 19–58

B

Bache, Richard 18, 21
Bache, Sarah 52
Barlow, Joel 87, 88, 92, 105
Bell, Robert 29, 34
Bevis, Dr John 9
Biddle, Owen 47, 57
Blake, William 83
Bonaparte, Napoleon, 100–1

Bonneville, Nicolas de 99, 100–1, 105–6
Bordentown 43, 56, 58, 60, 61, 104
Bowles, John 77
   A Protest against Tom Paine's Rights of Man 77
'Boston Massacre', the 20
'Boston Tea Party', the 20
Brissot de Wareville, 86
Bromley 82
Bryan, George 49
Bunker Hill, Battle of 26
Burgoyne, General John 43
Burke, Edmund 61, 63, 66–8, 69–71, 76–7, 79–81
   Reflections on the Revolution in France 67–8
Burr, Aaron 97

C

Calais 85

Chalmers, George ('Francis Oldys')
72
*Life of Thomas Pain; the Author of
the Rights of Men, with a Defence
of his Writings* 72

Chapman, Thomas 77

Chastellux, Marquis de 51–2

Christie, Thomas 66, 73, 87

Clootz, Anacharis 89, 93

Clymer, George 24

Cobbett, William 106 ·

Condorcet, Marquis de 62, 66, 74,
89
Appeal from the Old to the New
Whigs 76
*Answer to Four Questions on
the Legislative and Executive
Powers* (with Paine) 75

Cornwallis, General Charles 38

D

Danton, Georges-Jacques 86, 89,
93

Deane, Silas 44–5, 46, 52

Declaratory Act 1766 20

Declaration of Independence 37–8

Dover 9–10

E

Erskine, Thomas 84

F

Ferguson, James 9, 12

Fitzgerald, Lord 87

Fox, Charles James 64, 67, 82

France 38, 44–5, 48, 51, 52–3,

Franklin, Benjamin , 12, 18, 24–5, 29,
36, 46, 60–1, 91

Franklin, William 18

French Revolution, the 65–101

G

Gage, General Thomas 20, 23, 25

George III 12, 14, 16, 20–1, 24, 26–7, 30,
31, 64

Godwin, William 67, 69, 76

Grafton, Duke of 4

Grantham 12

Greene, General Nathaniel 38, 50

H

Hall, John 61

Hamilton, Alexander 83, 97, 104

Henry, William 43

Howe, Lord 40, 43

J

Jarvis, John Wesley 105

Jay, John 97, 104

Jefferson, Thomas 29, 36, 37, 66, 72, 91,
92, 97, 101, 102

Jones, John Paul 48

Jordan, J S 69, 77, 82

K

King of Prussia (privateer) 8

Kirkbride, Colonel Joseph 43, 56, 57,
58, 104

Knowles, Rev. William 5–6

L

Lafayette, Marquis de 52, 53, 62, 65–6,
67, 73, 78

Lambert, Mary (first wife) 10

Laurens, Henry 51, 61

Laurens, Colonel John 51, 53

Le Roy, Jean-Baptiste 62

Lee, Richard 36

Lewes (Suusex) 13–18

Lexington 25, 30, 42, 57

Livingstone, Robert 53

Locke, John 34, 91

London 7–9, 12, 63–4, 75–8

Louis XVI 56, 65, 73, 74–5, 88

M
Macdonald, Archibald 84
Madison, James 58, 72, 83, 95, 97
Marat, Jean Paul 88
Margate 10
Marshall, John 97
Martin, Benjamin 9
Monroe, James 93, 95, 105
Morris, Gouverneur 66, 67, 78, 84, 85, 92
Morris, Robert 47, 49, 53, 55

N
New Rochelle 58, 60, 89, 104, 105, 106
New York 24, 36, 38, 58, 60, 104–6
North, Lord 20

O
Ollive, Elizabeth (second wife) 16, 17–18
Ollive, Samuel 13, 16

P
Pain, Elizabeth (sister) 4
Pain, Frances (mother) 4, 63
Pain, Joseph (father) 4, 5, 6, 8, 63
Paine, Thomas
    America 18, 19–52, 53–61, 102–6
    appearance and manner 13, 36, 43, 51–2, 56, 63–4, 73, 76, 87, 103
    birth and early life 3–6
    bridge design 60–1, 62–3, 64, 67
    death 105–6
    drinking habits 16, 22, 42, 43, 88, 92, 100, 101, 104, 105
    excise officer 11–12, 13–17
    France 52–3, 61–2, 66–7, 72–3, 74–5, 84, 85–101
    French National Assembly, member of 85–9, 94
    Great Britain 3–18, 62–4, 75–8, 82–4
    imprisonment 89, 92–3
    inventions 42, 43, 60–1

marriages 10, 16–18, 25, 72
military career 38–9, 43
privateering 7–8
publications:
    Agrarian Justice 98–9, 103
    Answer to Four Questions on the Legislative and Executive Powers (with Condorcet) 75
    Common Sense 28–32, 33–5, 41, 45, 50, 56, 71, 81, 92
    Dissertation on First Principles of Government 94
    Dissertations on Government; the Affairs of the Bank; and Paper Money 59
    'Farmer Short's Dog Porter: A Tale' (poem) 15
    Letter of Thomas Paine to the People of France 86
    Letter to the Abbé Raynal, on the Affairs of North America 56
    Observations on the Construction and Operation of Navies with a Plan for an Invasion of England and the Final Overthrow of the English Government 100
    Plain Truth, see *Common Sense*
    Prospects on the Rubicon 63
    Public Good 51
    'Reflections on Unhappy Marriages' (article) 25
    Rights of Man, Part 1 68, 69–73, 76, 92
    Rights of Man, Part 2 75, 76, 78, 79–81, 98, 103
    The Age of Reason 10, 90–2, 94, 102
    The American Crisis 1 39–40, 104
    The American Crisis 2 40
    The American Crisis 3 42
    The American Crisis 4 42
    The American Crisis 5 43

The American Crisis 6 44
The American Crisis 7 45
The American Crisis 8 48
The American Crisis 9 49
The American Crisis 10 55
The American Crisis 12 75
The American Crisis 13 57, 75
The Case of the Officers of Excise
 16–17, 98
The Crisis Extraordinary 50–1
The Decline and Fall of the
 English System of Finance 96
'Thoughts on a Defensive War'
 (article) 26
To the Citizens of the United
 States 103
religion 5, 10, 13, 90–2, 94, 99, 103–4,
 105–6
scientific studies 9, 10, 58, 60
Secretary to the Committee of
 Foreign Affairs (US) 42–5
slavery 24, 37, 49
social security 80–1
staymaker 7, 8, 9
teacher 12
Paris 65–7, 73
Philadelphia 21–2, 103
Pitt, William (the Younger) 64, 82–3
Priestley, Joseph 66, 76, 83, 103

Q
Quakers, the 5, 8, 26, 105–6
Quartering Act 1765

R
Randolph, Edmund 72
Raynal, Abbé Guillaume 56

Rickman, Thomas 'Clio' 13, 76, 84, 88,
 101, 103, 105
Rittenhouse, David 24, 27, 42, 47
Robespierre, Maximilien 86, 89, 91, 93
Romney, George 76
Rush, Benjamin 24–5, 28–9, 47, 103

S
Saratoga 43
Seven Years War, The 7, 19
Sharp, William 76, 82
St Just, Louis-Antoine de 86, 89
Stamp Act 1765
Sugar Act 1764 19

T
Terrible (privateer) 7–8
Thetford 4–6, 12, 13, 60, 63
Took, John Horne 76
Treaty of Paris, the 58
Trumbull, John 62

V
Vasse, Cornélie de 64

W
Washington, George 25, 34, 38, 57, 67,
 83, 91, 94, 96, 97, 104
Watson, Elkanah 53
Wilkes, John 13–14, 63
Witherspoon, Dr John 21–2, 52
Wollstonecraft, Mary 67, 68, 76, 88, 100
 A Vindication of the Rights of Man
  68
 A Vindication of the Rights of Women
  68
Wordsworth, William 87